DRAWN FROM 2017

The year in cartoons

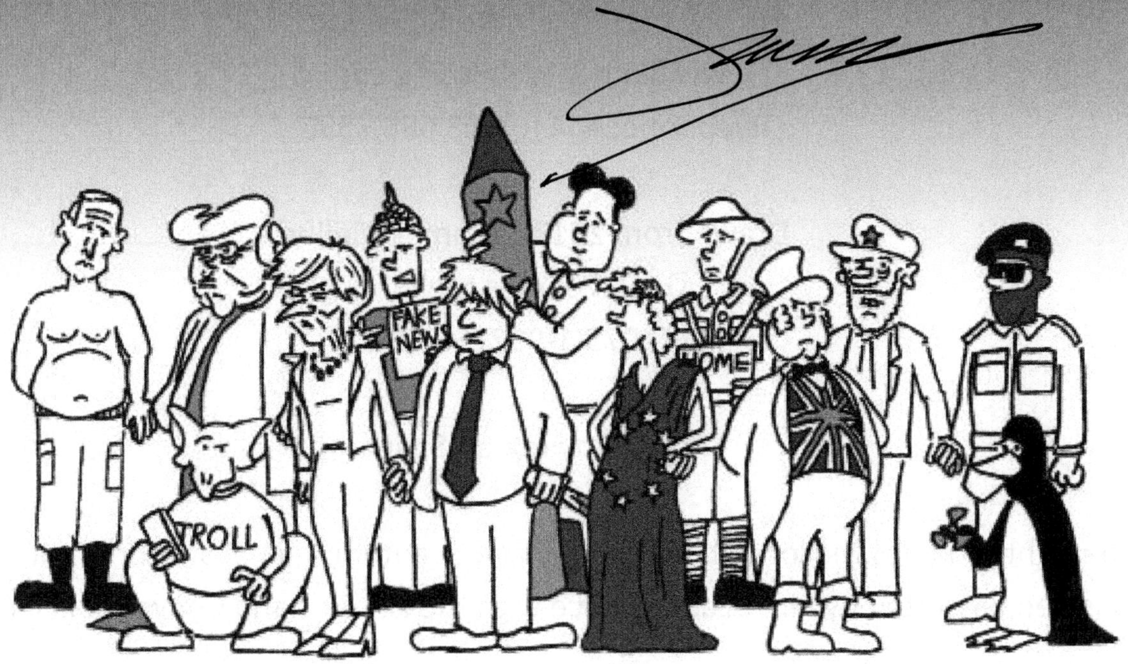
FAKE NEWS
HOME
TROLL

James Mellor

with Foreword from International Chess Grandmaster, Raymond Keene OBE

Published by
Filament Publishing Ltd
16 Croydon Road, Beddington, Croydon,
Surrey, CR0 4PA, United Kingdom.
www.filamentpublishing.com
Telephone: +44 (0)208 688 2598

Drawn from 2017 by James Mellor
© 2017 James Mellor
ISBN 978-1-912256-53-2

Printed by IngramSpark

What people are saying about James Mellor's 'Drawn from History'

I love this book; bringing history to life through cartoons is genius.
Greg Wallace - Host of BBC's Time Commanders and Masterchef

A great book that will have you chuckling out loud as you browse dozens of splendidly witty cartoons.
This England Magazine

A hysterical history of a nations finest, and not so finest hours.
The Reigatian

His work simultaneously pokes fun at the past whilst celebrating it and provides an entertaining opportunity for readers to engage with history.
OVL Magazine

You've got Knight fever, Knight fe-ver

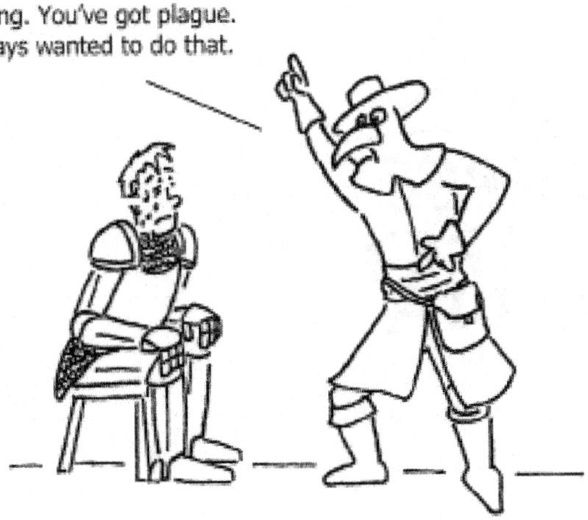
Only kidding. You've got plague.
I just always wanted to do that.

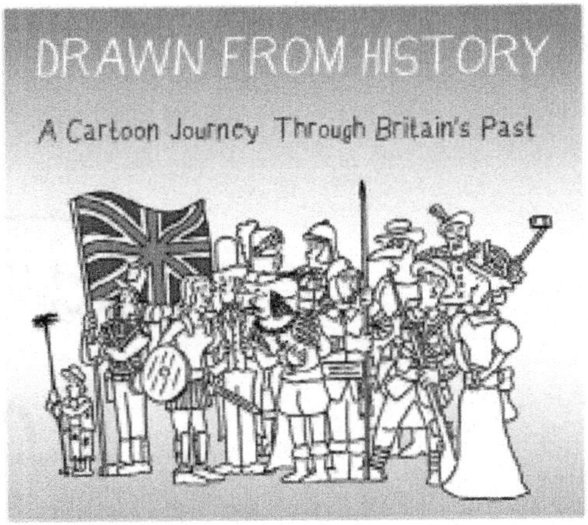
DRAWN FROM HISTORY
A Cartoon Journey Through Britain's Past

NOW ON SALE

I am fortunate enough to live in a country where I am free to do my job. Not every cartoonist enjoys this freedom. Below is my cartoon from this year's #FreeTurkeyMedia campaign.

Turkey is just one of many countries which have cracked down on, imprisoned and prosecuted cartoonists merely for doing their jobs by holding those in power to account. You can find out their stories and ways you can help here:

amnesty.org.uk

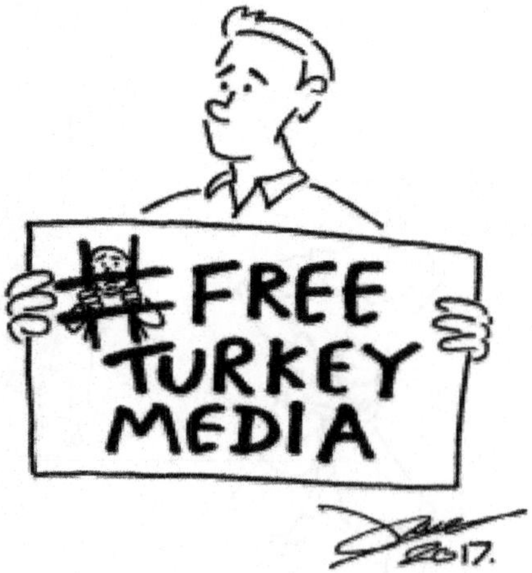
#FREE TURKEY MEDIA
2017.

About the author

James Mellor is a freelance writer and cartoonist. He launched his company James Mellor Creative in 2012 to help people turn their ideas into usable, engaging and memorable content. The business is built around his three areas of expertise – research, writing and cartoon illustration – deployed either independently or in combination. In these areas, he has worked with large institutions, SMEs, start-ups and individuals to get their unique messages across in print, online and via social media.

In his illustrative role, James creates cartoons for a wide range of corporate and private clients. Outside of JMC, he is the Associate Illustrator at Lea Graham Associates Ltd. His cartoon work also appears regularly in Professional & Organisational Development's Thought for the Week and GAMBICA's Business Impacts. A History graduate from the University of York, James' main interest away from work is the past (which probably comes across in his cartoons). As a supporter of Harlequins and Arsenal, he is accustomed to long periods of disappointment punctuated by occasional moments of brilliance.

James lives in Rushden with his wife Rachel, daughter Talitha, and a small, sociopathic cat.

w: jamesmellorcreative.com t: @jamesdfmellor f: jamesmellorcreative

Acknowledgements

This book is quite different from my last. At least, it is very different when it comes to writing acknowledgements. There have been many people involved and there are many to thank. Much of the work featured was created in collaboration with clients – thank you all very much.

I am very grateful that you choose to use my pictures to convey your messages and I thank you for the inspiration and guidance. I have worked with some of you since I first set up shop in 2012 and I value your long-term support. Others of you I am just starting to illustrate for and get to know; I hope we are able to establish similar lasting connections.

Thank you to Rachel for your constant love and support, for helping me through the creative process and for being an excellent judge of good taste in cartoons (especially for notifying me when I have exceeded it). I must also thank little Talitha, who provides the ultimate motivation for me to succeed, occasionally provides inspiration and, every once in a while, goes to sleep long enough for me to get some drawing done.

I grudgingly thank the cat, though I fail to fully understand why.

Foreword
Raymond Keene OBE

As James Mellor notes in his new anthology of life, the universe and everything, taken from the annals of 2017, he is fortunate to live under a system which treats cartoonists with both toleration and good humour. Targets of the cartoonists' barbs tend to purchase the original work of their tormentors, rather than persecute them. Cartoonists elsewhere have not been so lucky, witness murderous extremist attacks on editorial offices in Paris in recent years, where the slaughter of Charlie Hebdo artists and staff led to a mass international movement in support of those who exercise their right both to free speech and free sketch. Elsewhere , cartoonists have been suppressed, silenced and even sentenced.

Licence to lampoon, in the UK at least, goes back to Hogarth, Gillray and Rowlandson in the 18th century, who, in their visual productions, echoed the satirical writings of Aristophanes, Juvenal and Martial from the days of Ancient Greece and Rome. Targets of satire have traditionally been politicians, rulers, social fads, celebrities and the morals and mores of the period. The reigning Monarch of Gillray's time, King George II , may have writhed under the castigatory cartoons of the draughtsmen of the day, but the temptation to retaliate was universally resisted. Lese Majeste was regarded with toleration, not torture, a fortiori from that Hanoverian scion, Prinny, George IV, the gluttonously rotund "fat friend" of Beau Brummell, a cartoonists' gift and notorious butt of the colourfully acerbic quill.

James Mellor operates within that tradition, elegantly excoriating the pretensions of politics, the foibles of fashion and the excessive eccentricities of celebrities and the news. Mild mockery, decisive draughtsmanship and creative content characterise Mellor's Pages, and if Memory is the warder of the brain, as Shakespeare put it, then this authorised version by James will help to cement the fads, foibles and fantasies of the year 2017 in the collective archival Memory Palace of years to come.

Ray Keene OBE
London
28 10 2017

Table of Contents

10

Introduction

We live in a Golden Age for cartoonists. So we're told. Certainly, material is abundant. It does feel as though we are living through historic times. Perhaps not sharp, distinct, historic moments, such as the fall of the Berlin Wall or the Moon landing, but more of a long, drawn-out process. Like an ongoing motorway pile-up. However, real life has become so cartoonish, it can be difficult to know how to cartoon it. Donald Trump, Kim Jong-un, Jeremy Corbyn, Boris Johnson and others don't just look rather cartoon-like, their words and actions can be as exaggerated and surreal as their visuals. Sometimes one wonders 'where can I take this?', as the situation is weird enough as it is. Fortunately, cartoons are not bounded by time, space or reality and there is always a new and hopefully amusing angle to see things from.

It helps that I've always covered a range of topics. Roughly speaking, my work to date has been focussed on business, politics and history. These areas have become increasingly intertwined. The business world seems more political, and filled with more people who recognise the value, lessons and relevance of history. I receive corporate commissions asking me to make a political point using a historical setting or event as a metaphor. I like this. Please don't worry, my work remains just as silly as it ever was. Just, perhaps, slightly more focussed. Rest assured that as you turn the pages, you will still find cheap jokes, puns, wordplay and, yes, you will still find a few penguins. I hope you enjoy the cartoons.

James.

"You're Joking? Not another one!"*

UK News

The producers of 2017 decided to continue last year's divisive Brexit story arc – even ratcheting the situation up a notch with the passing of Article 50. Having argued whether or not to vote for 'something else', the nation is now arguing over what 'something else' actually means.

In the midst of this (and partly because of it), a surprise election was called, a surprisingly bad campaign was run by the Conservatives and a surprisingly good, though ultimately unsuccessful, result achieved by their Labour opponents.

Unsurprisingly, we're left with a mess. The unsustainable ones narrowly beat the unelectable ones, neither party wholeheartedly supports its own leadership and, it seems, no-one is any clearer to knowing what 'something else' really is. But we keep calm and carry on. Because we're British and that's what it says on the posters and mugs.

*Brenda

Why are we voting?

The regions of the UK didn't all vote
the same way in the EU referendum,
then the regions of Scotland didn't all
vote the same way in their referendum,
then the consituencies within the Scottish
regions didn't all vote the same way in the next,
and...well, we've just worked our way down since

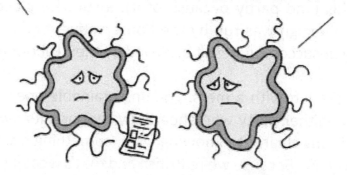

Bacterial Referendum 2056
(should the head or the heart get to cast the vote for this
individual's body in the household vote on independence)

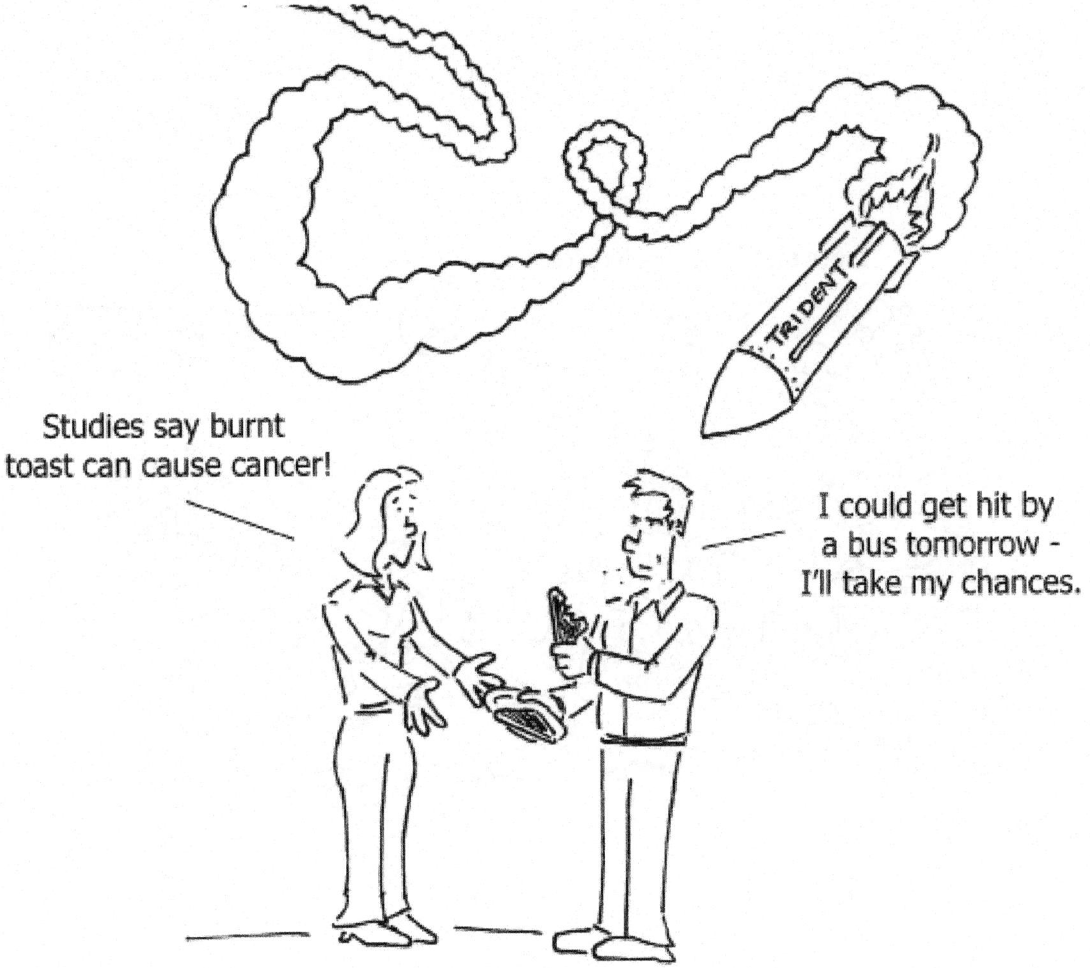
TRIDENT
Studies say burnt toast can cause cancer!
I could get hit by a bus tomorrow - I'll take my chances.

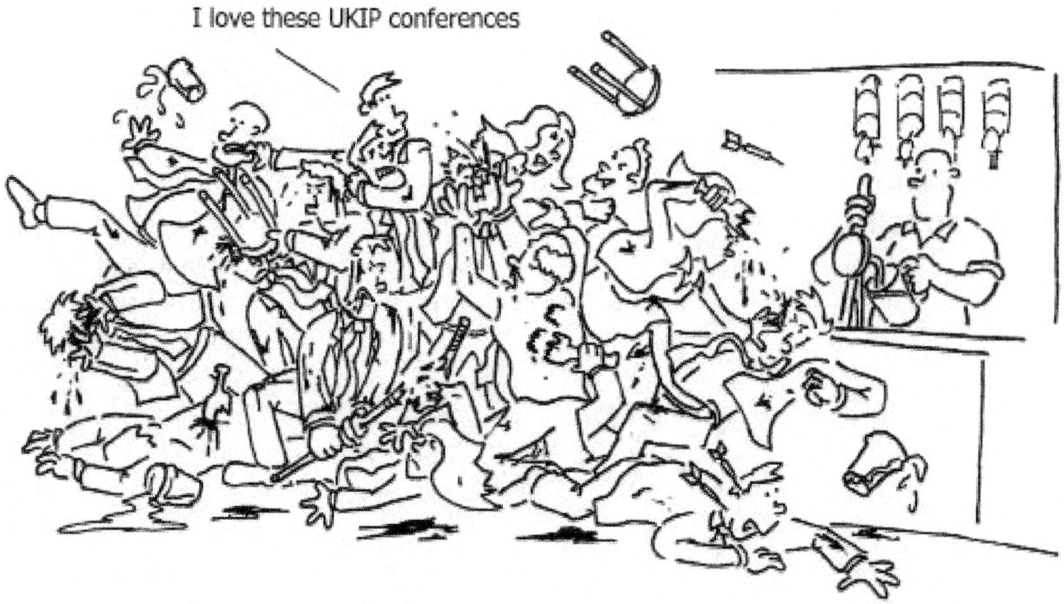
I love these UKIP conferences

If he's worried about being spied on, one thing he could try is to *stop meeting with people* who we *definitely are* spying on

GCHQ

Universal Brexit Cartoon

Remain voters: cover up everything right of the vertical line

Leave voters: cover up the caption below the horizontal line

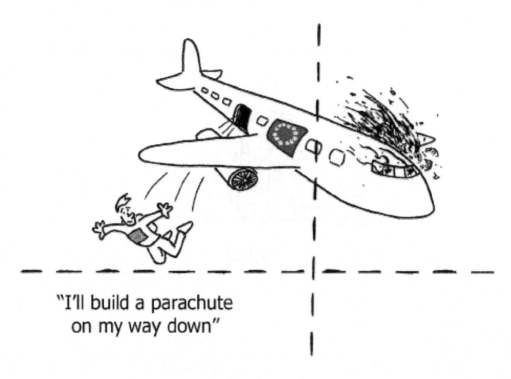

"I'll build a parachute
on my way down"

War with Spain?

No, Smith!
Don't charge the red rag
- it's a trick!

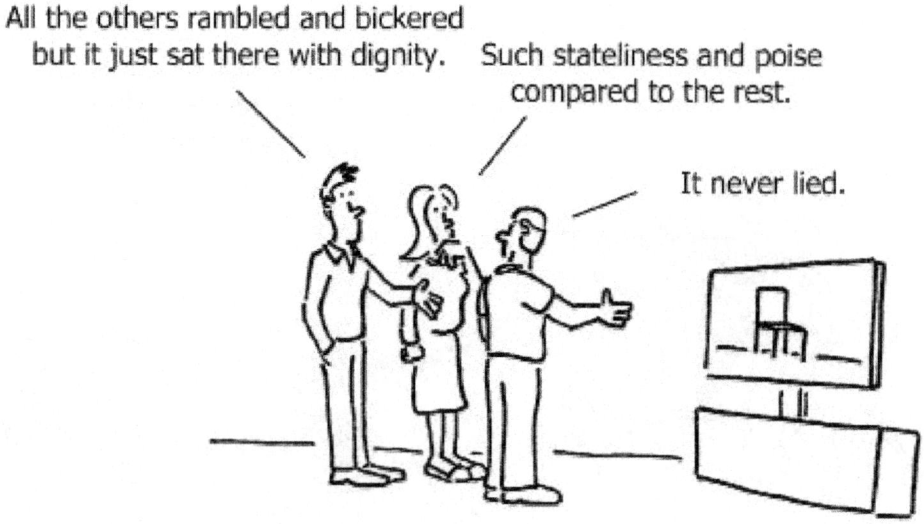
All the others rambled and bickered but it just sat there with dignity.
Such stateliness and poise compared to the rest.
It never lied.

'Empty Chair' proves a surprise hit in TV Election Debates

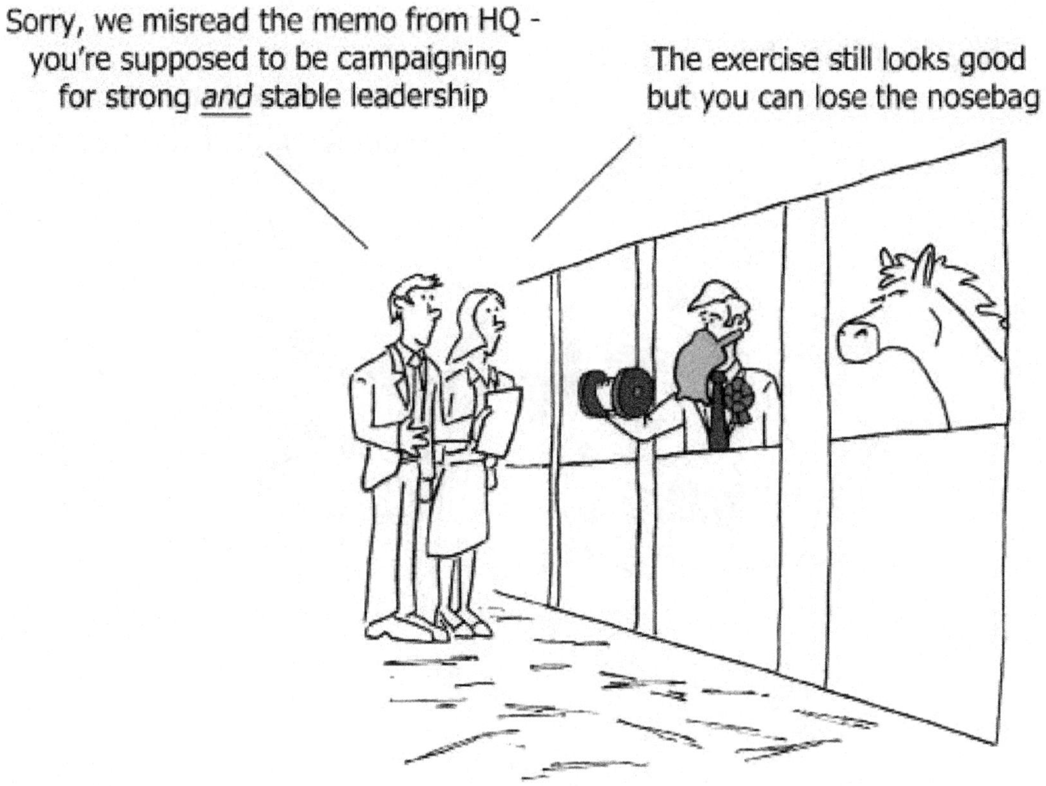
Sorry, we misread the memo from HQ - you're supposed to be campaigning for strong and stable leadership
The exercise still looks good but you can lose the nosebag

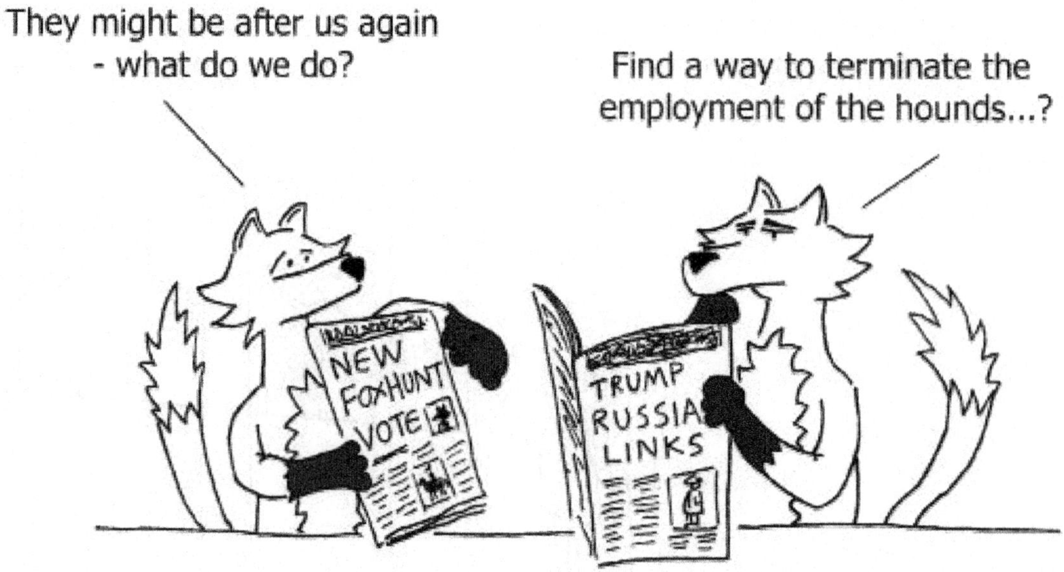
They might be after us again - what do we do?
Find a way to terminate the employment of the hounds...?
NEW FOXHUNT VOTE
TRUMP RUSSIA LINKS

If May wants to bring back foxhunting I guess
you'll be changing your support this election?
Have you seen the Labour front bench?
I'll take my chances with the hounds.

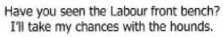

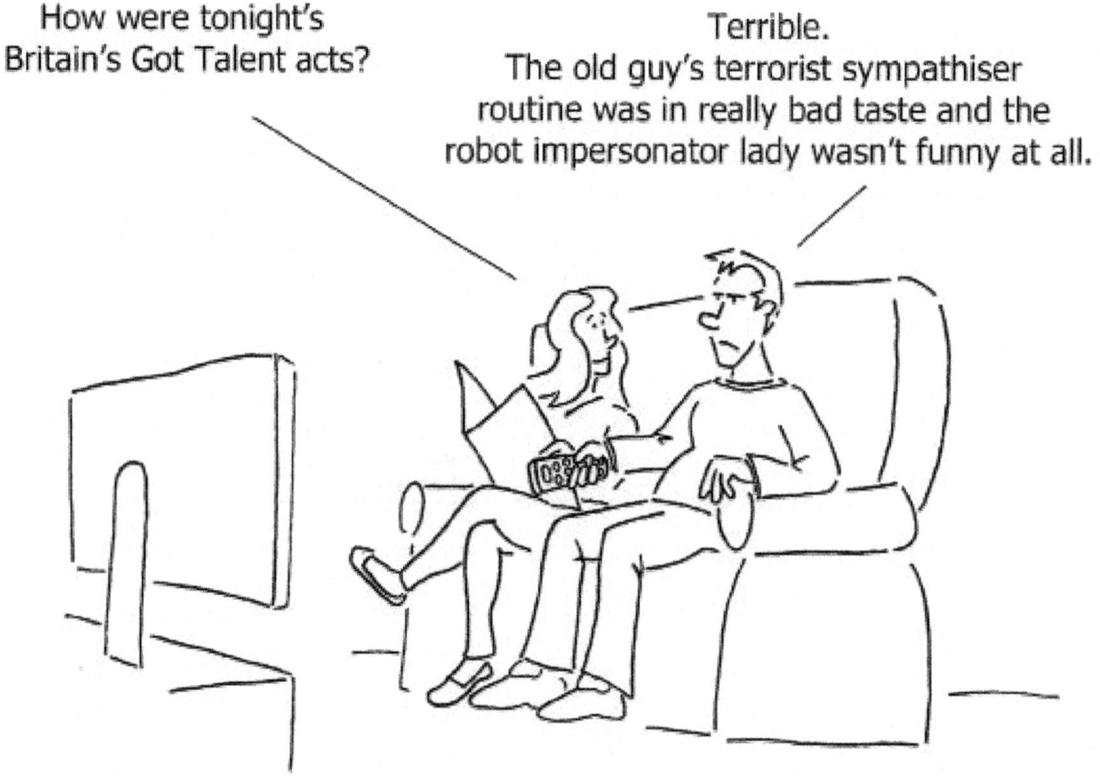
How were tonight's Britain's Got Talent acts?
Terrible. The old guy's terrorist sympathiser routine was in really bad taste and the robot impersonator lady wasn't funny at all.

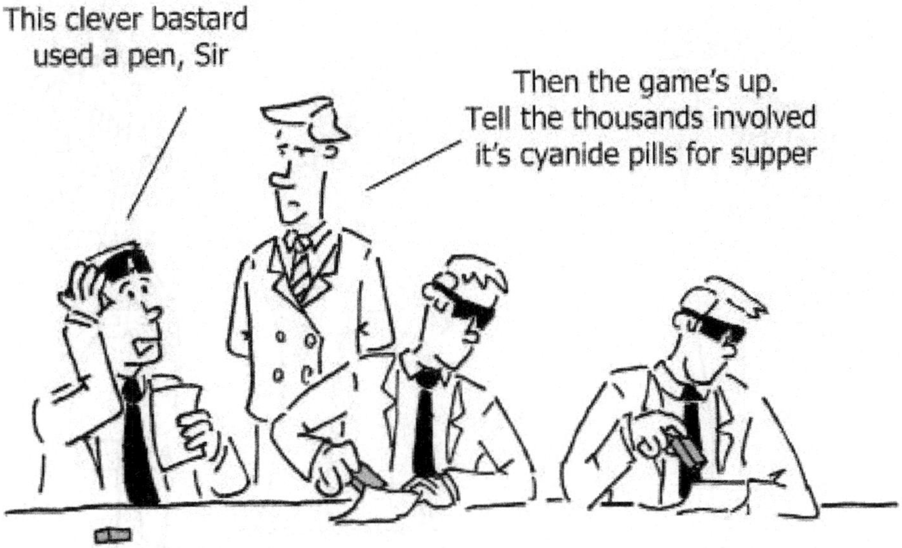
This clever bastard
used a pen, Sir
Then the game's up.
Tell the thousands involved
it's cyanide pills for supper

Top Secret MI5 Rubbing-Out Facility

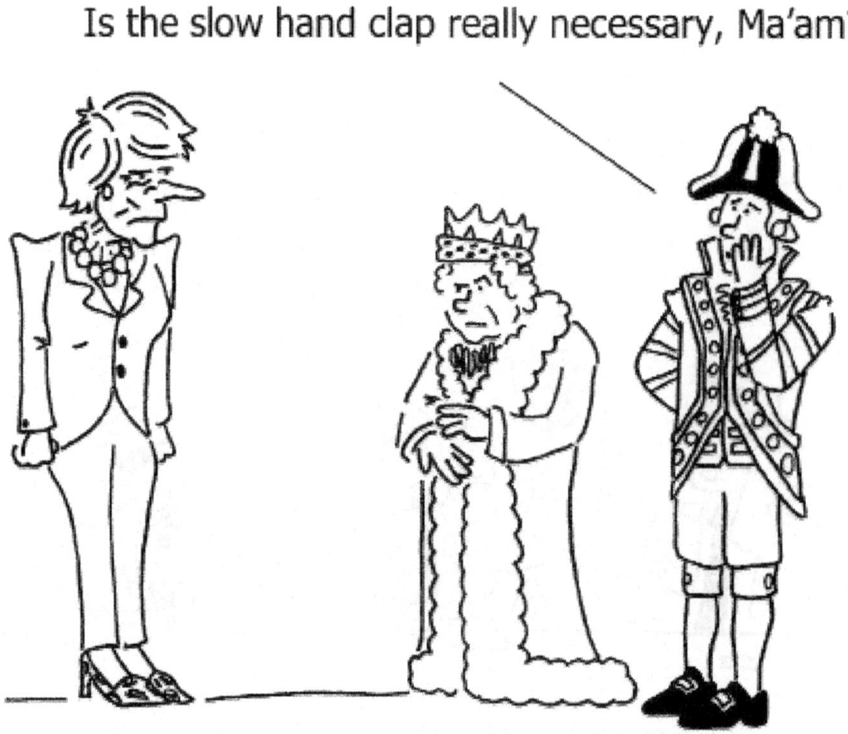
Is the slow hand clap really necessary, Ma'am?

Theresa May to ask Queen's permission to form government

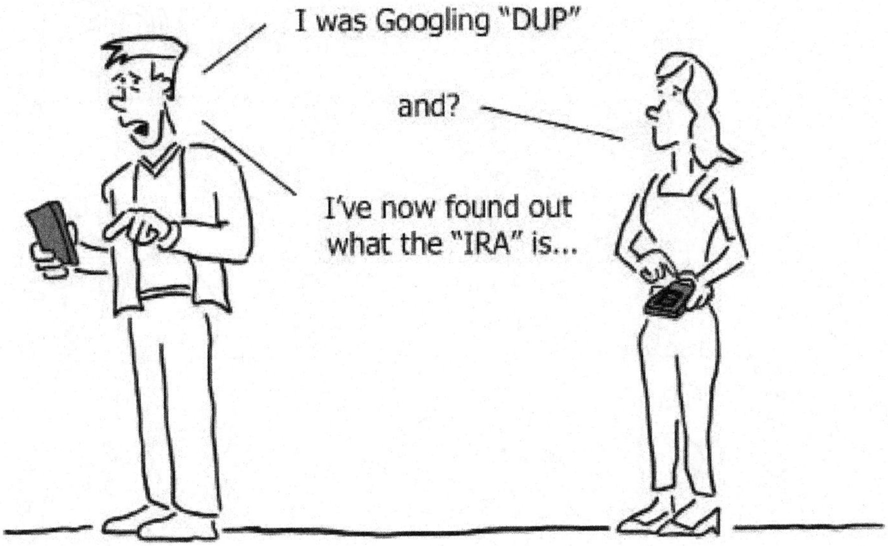
I was Googling "DUP"
and?
I've now found out what the "IRA" is...

Youth Vote

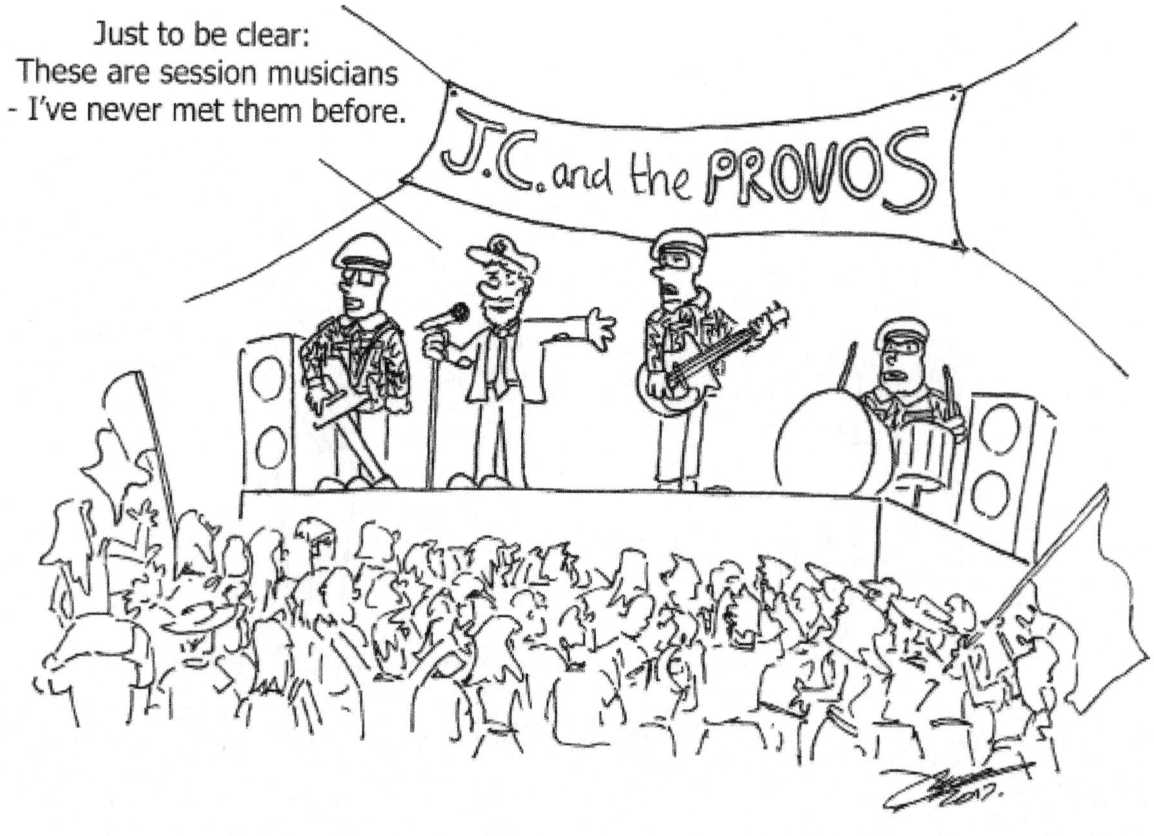

Just to be clear:
These are session musicians
- I've never met them before.
J.C. and the PROVOS

Let me see that

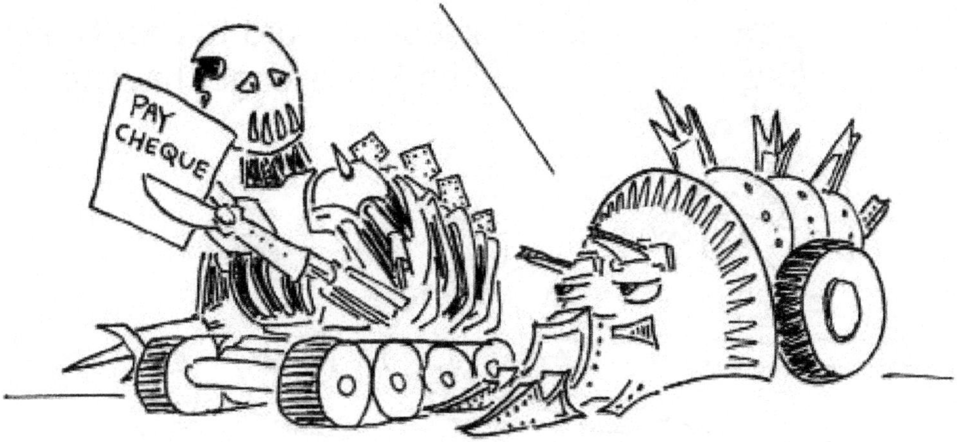
PAY
CHEQUE

BBC gender pay gap

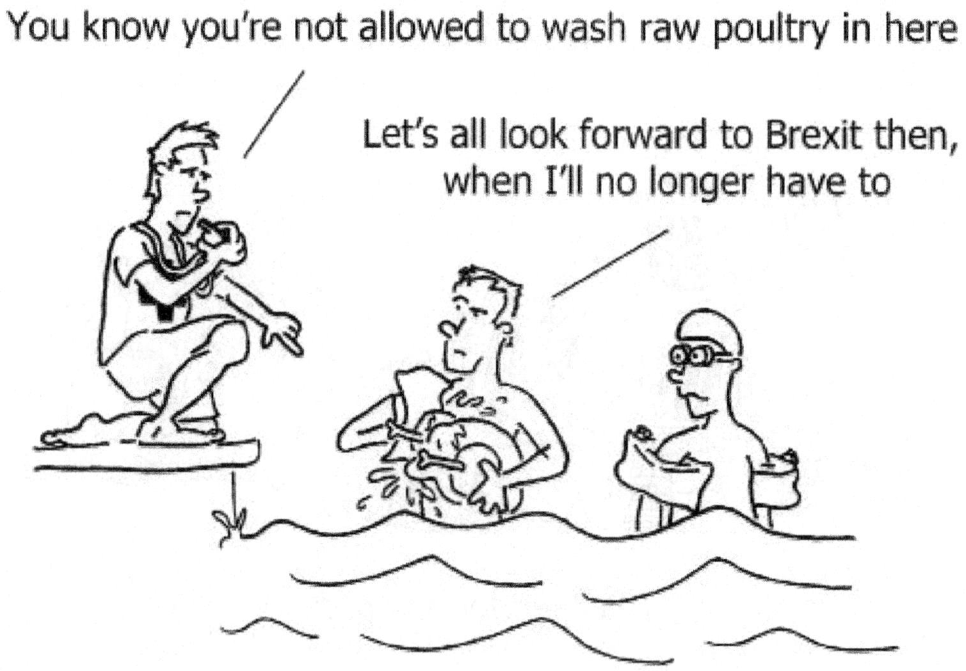
You know you're not allowed to wash raw poultry in here
Let's all look forward to Brexit then, when I'll no longer have to

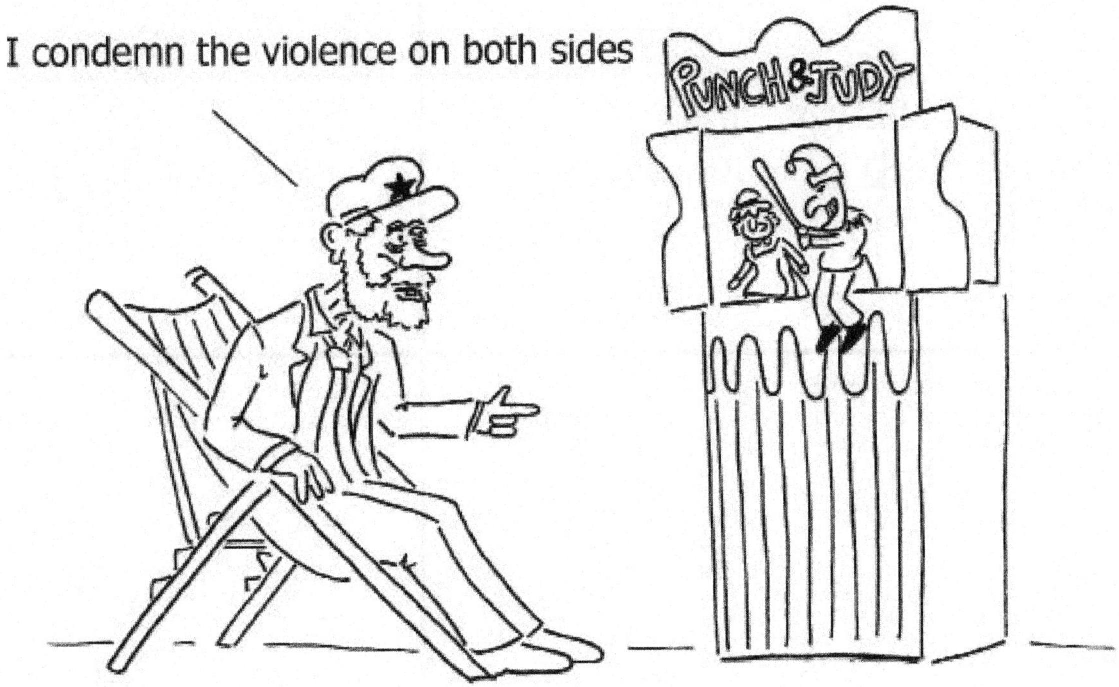
I condemn the violence on both sides
PUNCH&JUDY

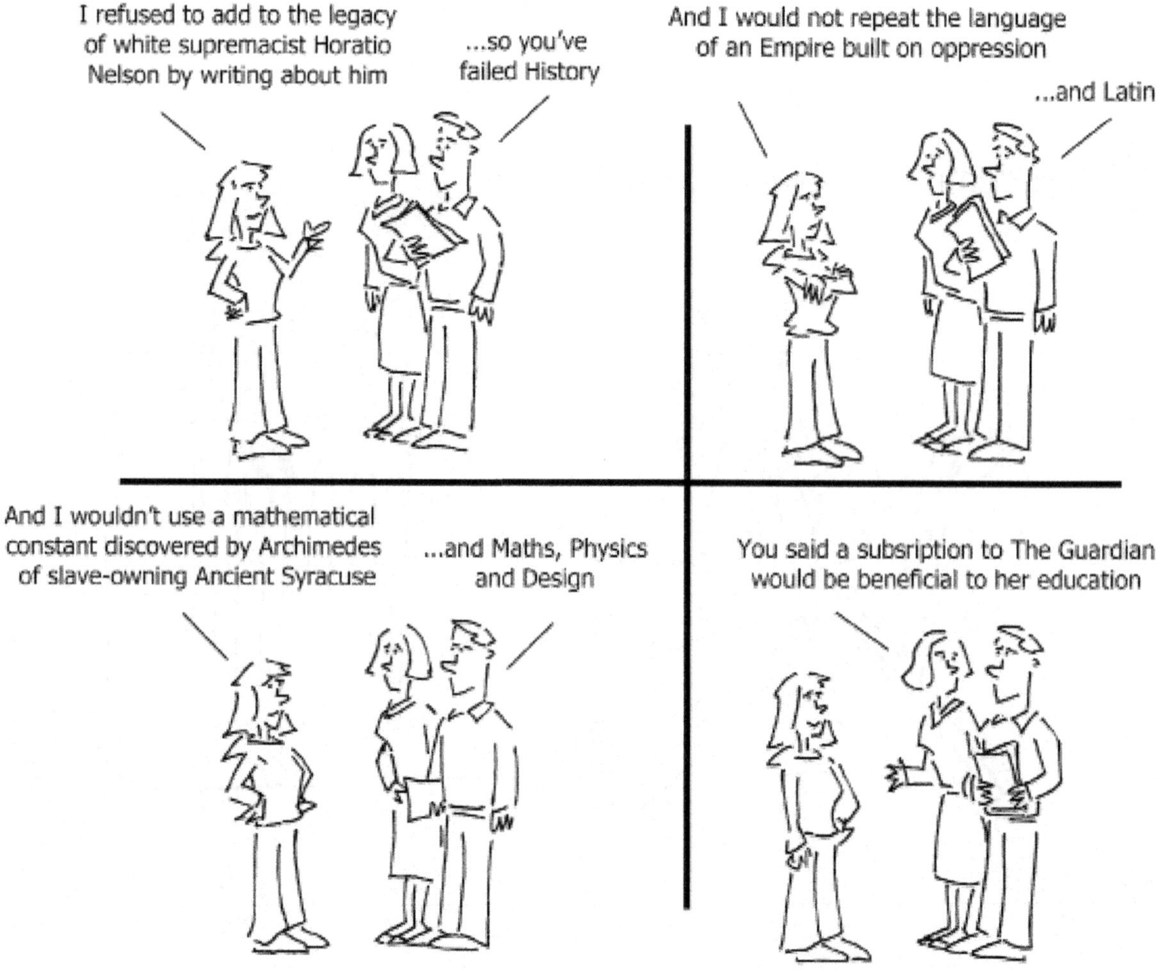
I refused to add to the legacy of white supremacist Horatio Nelson by writing about him
...so you've failed History
And I would not repeat the language of an Empire built on oppression
...and Latin
And I wouldn't use a mathematical constant discovered by Archimedes of slave-owning Ancient Syracuse
...and Maths, Physics and Design
You said a subsription to The Guardian would be beneficial to her education

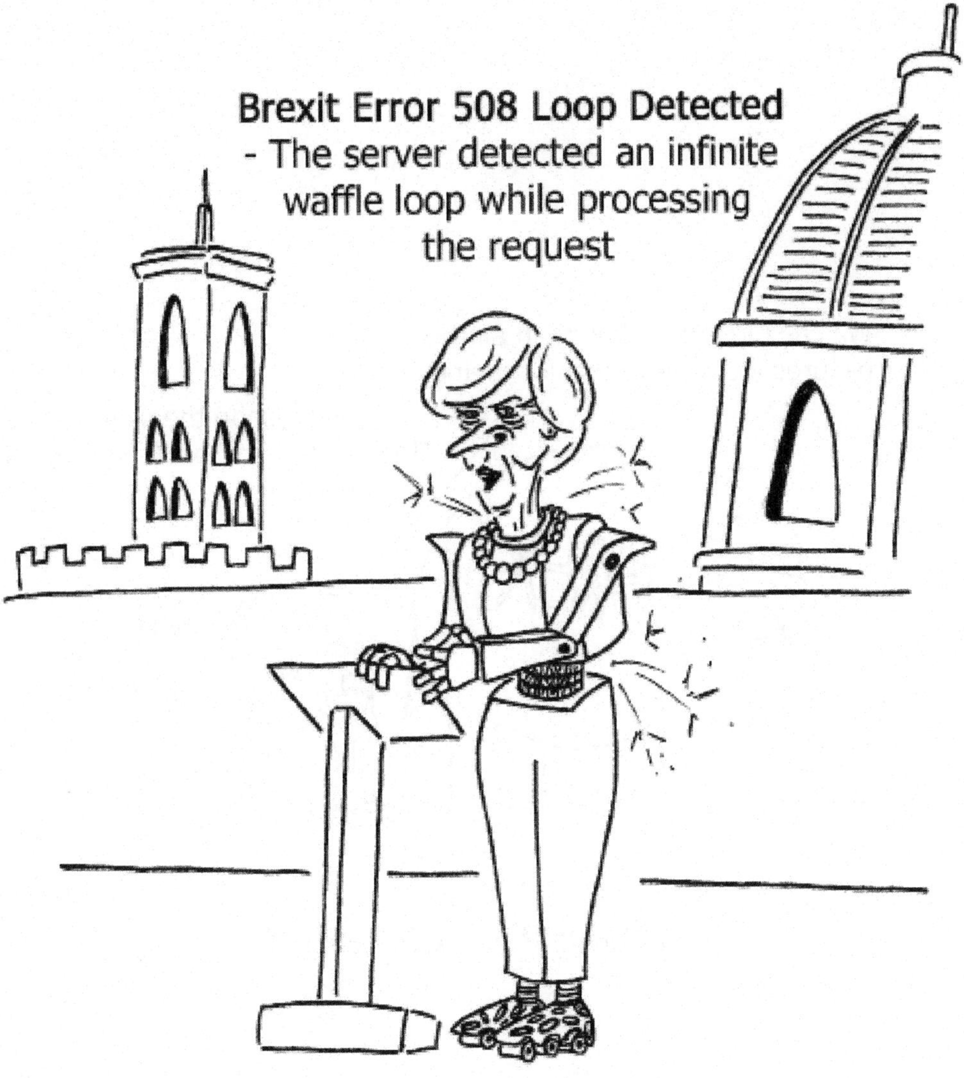
Brexit Error 508 Loop Detected
- The server detected an infinite waffle loop while processing the request

Florence and the Machine

We can't ignore it. It'll be in all the pictures we want to use for memes
Photoshop the side - 'Momentephant' or 'Trotskyderm'
Nice
BREXIT

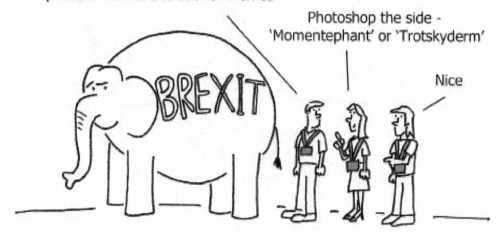

Labour Party Conference

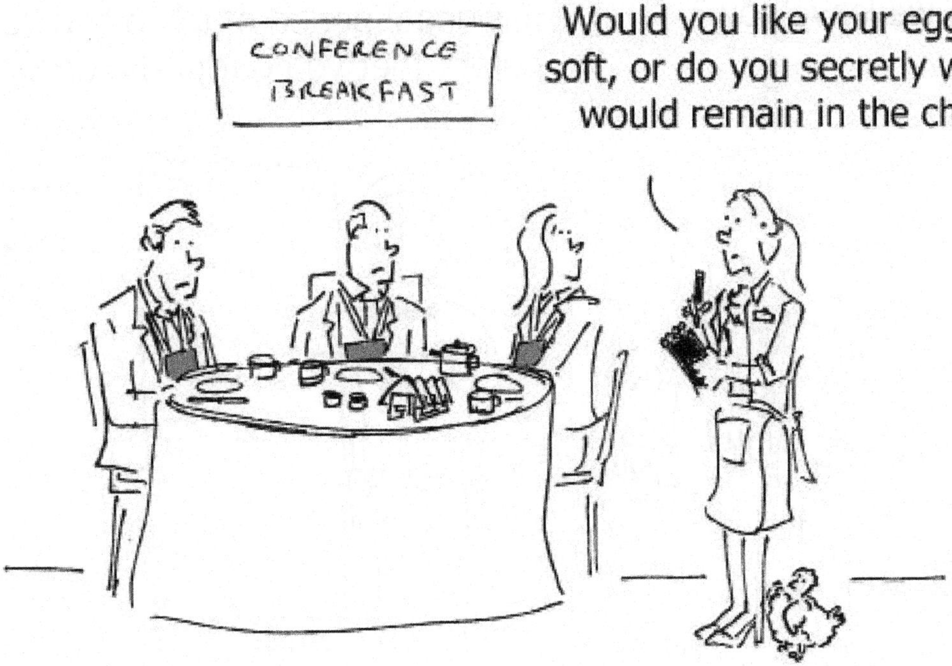
CONFERENCE
BREAKFAST

Would you like your eggs hard, soft, or do you secretly wish they would remain in the chicken?

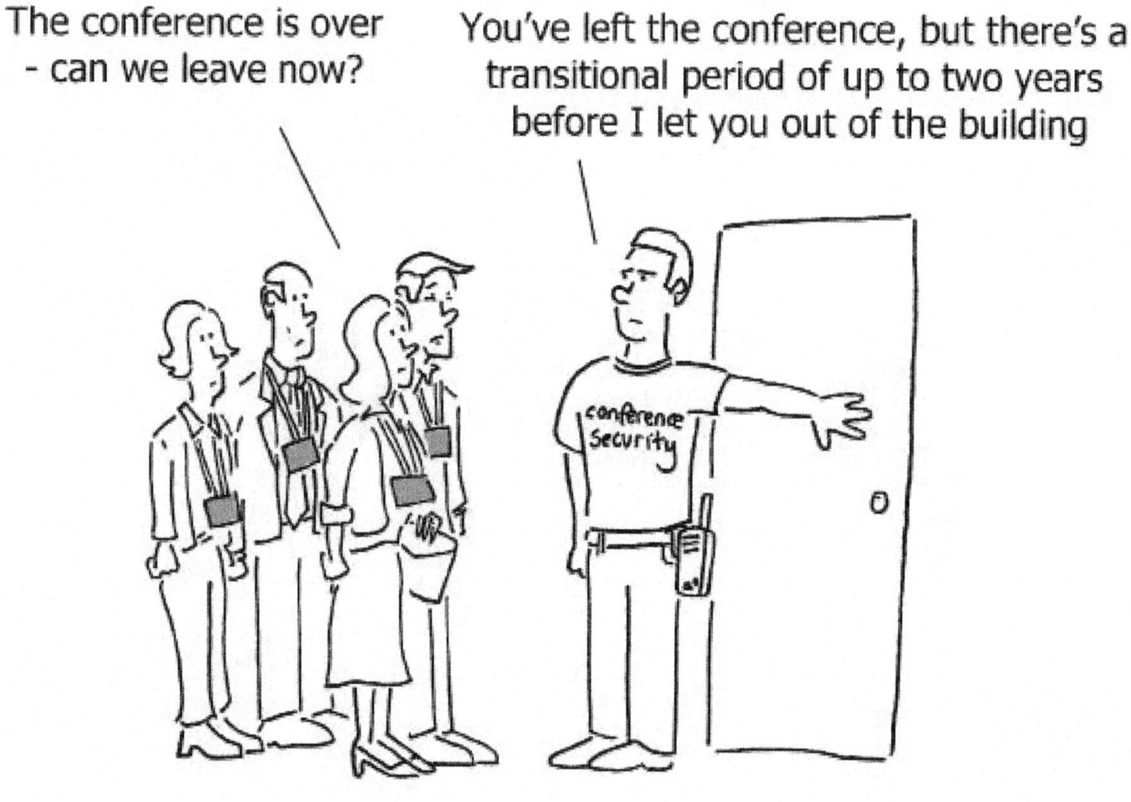
The conference is over - can we leave now?
You've left the conference, but there's a transitional period of up to two years before I let you out of the building
conference Security

Freshly ground daily grind

Cartoons for Business

The cartoons in this section were commissioned by clients and, as such, are drawn from the worlds of HR, Financial Services, Law, Consultancy, Engineering, FinTech and elsewhere. However, I feel that very few are narrowly sector specific.

The absurdities and frustrations of modern day professional life are often universal. The issues of decision making, delegation, and the elusive work/life balance affect us all.

Hopefully, we are able to see the amusing side of them too.

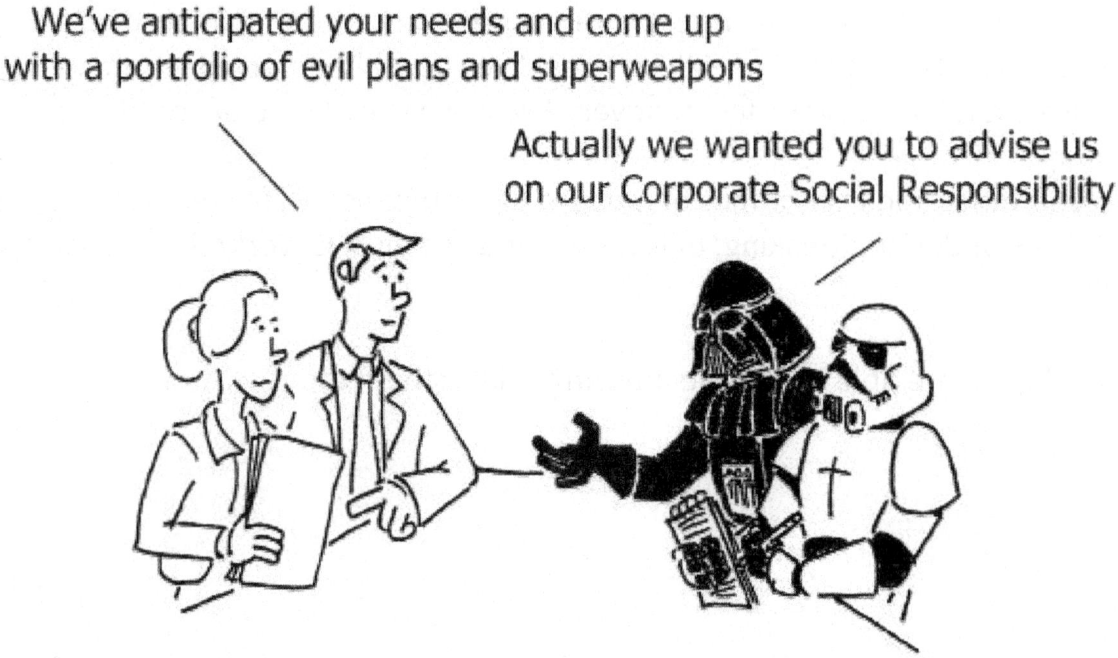
We've anticipated your needs and come up with a portfolio of evil plans and superweapons
Actually we wanted you to advise us on our Corporate Social Responsibility

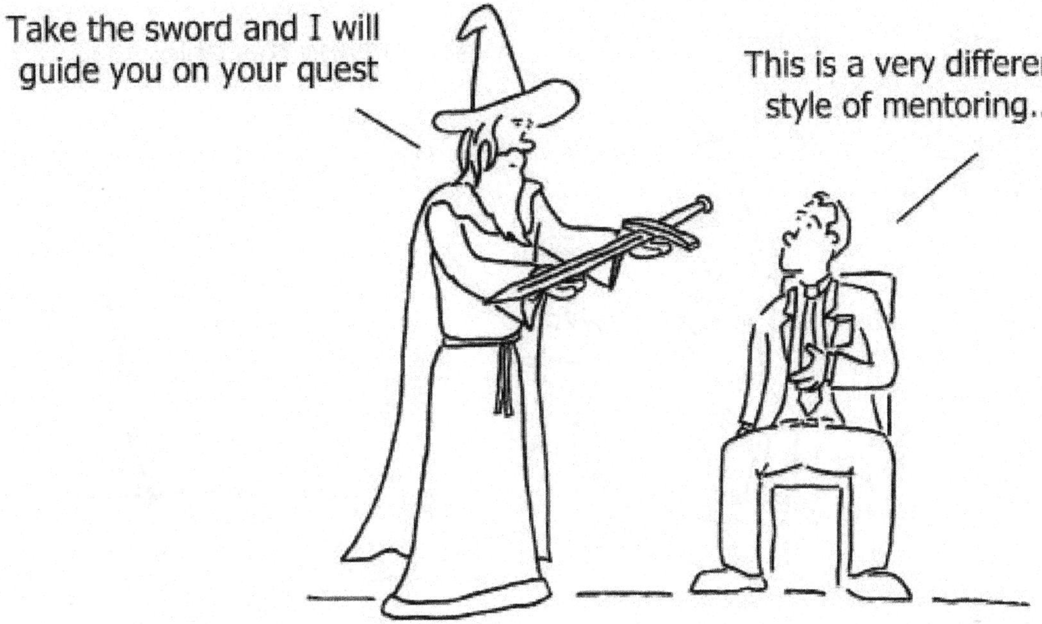
Take the sword and I will guide you on your quest
This is a very different style of mentoring...

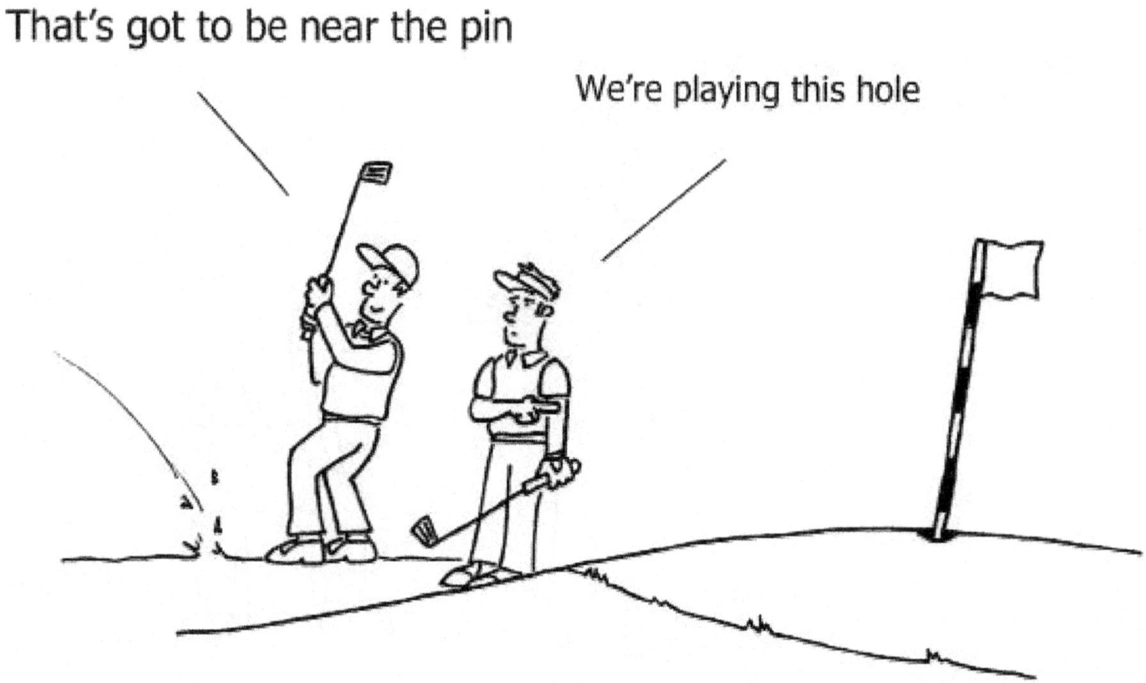
That's got to be near the pin
We're playing this hole

Did you know that 90% of an iceberg is below the waterline?
100% of *us* will be below the waterline if you hit one

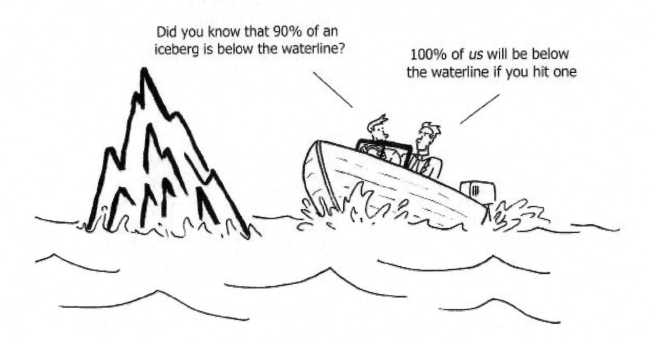

Hidden Dangers

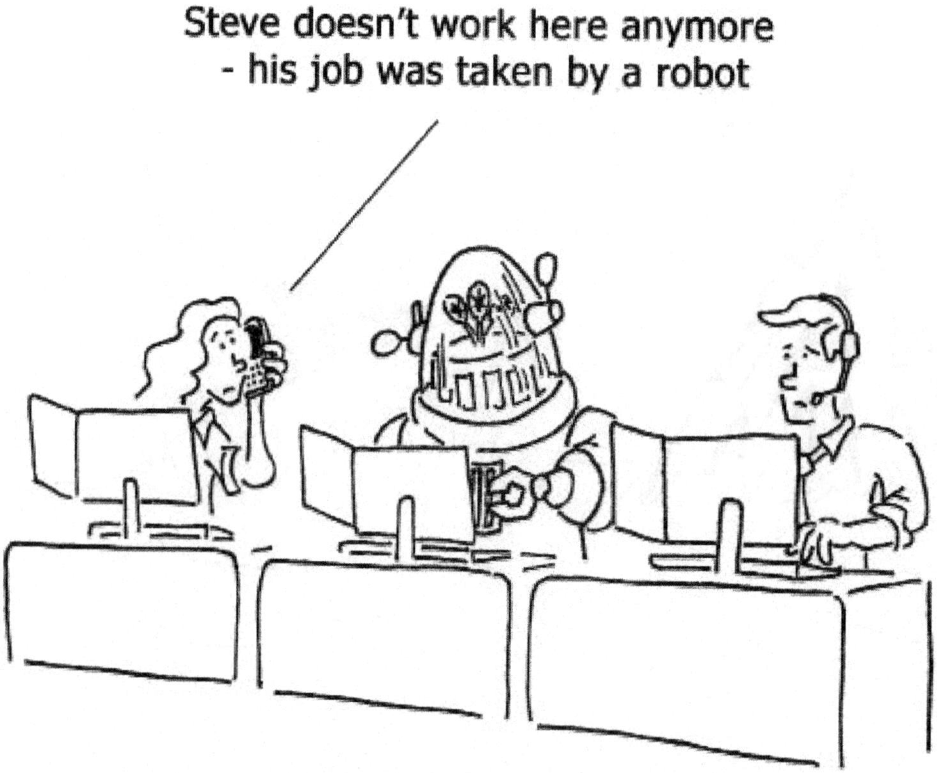
Steve doesn't work here anymore
- his job was taken by a robot

My calendar didn't sync properly with my phone.
Remind me - when am I supposed to 'beware'?

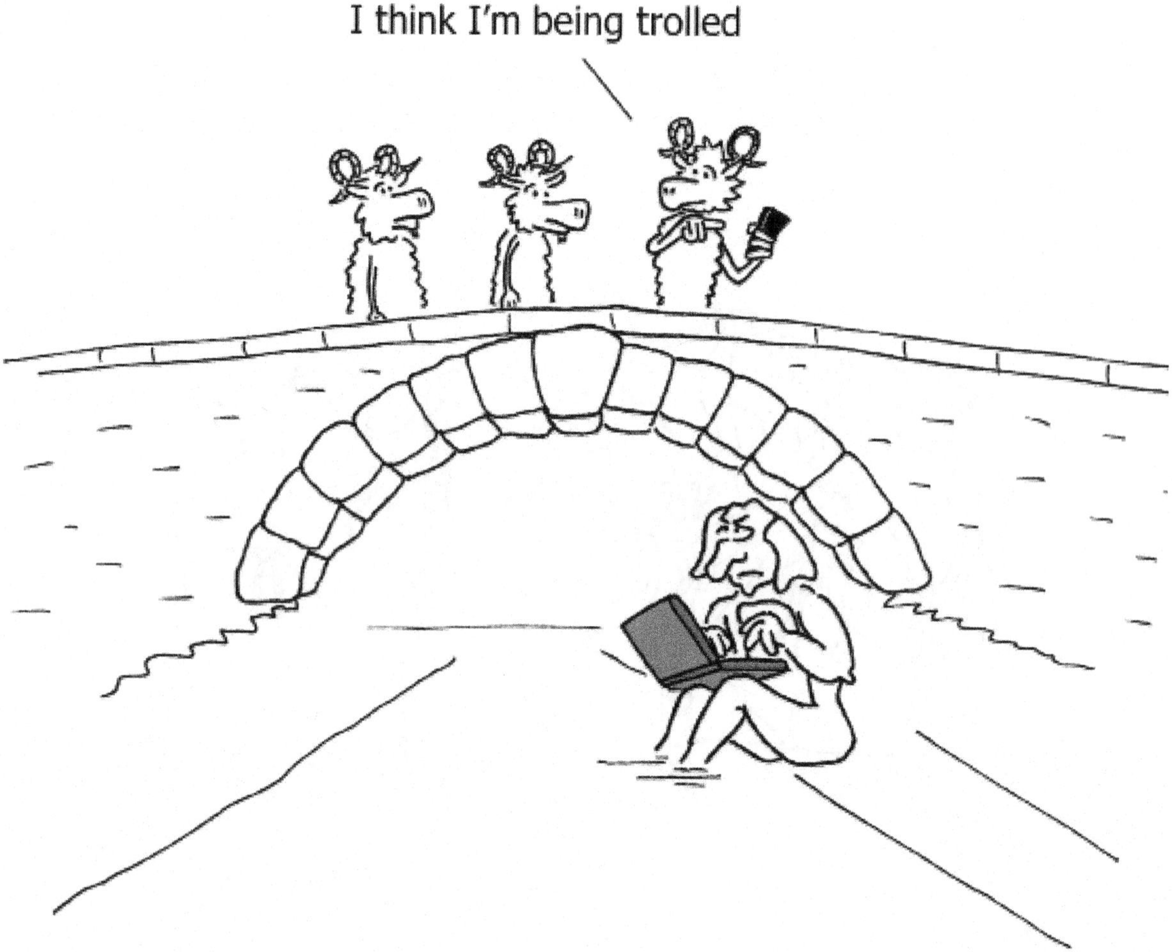
I think I'm being trolled

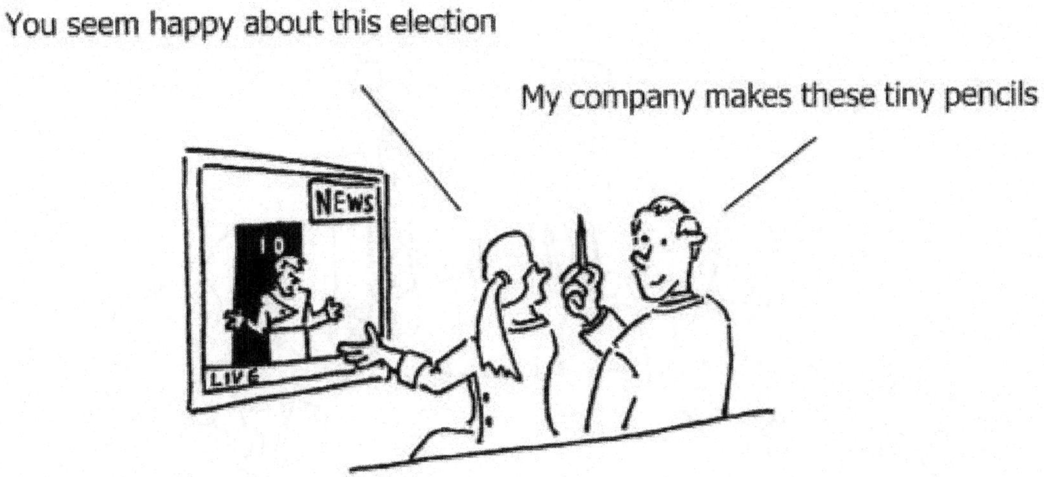
You seem happy about this election
My company makes these tiny pencils
NEWS
10
LIVE

The bad news is we don't know what to do.
The good news is we're *unanimously agreed* we don't know.

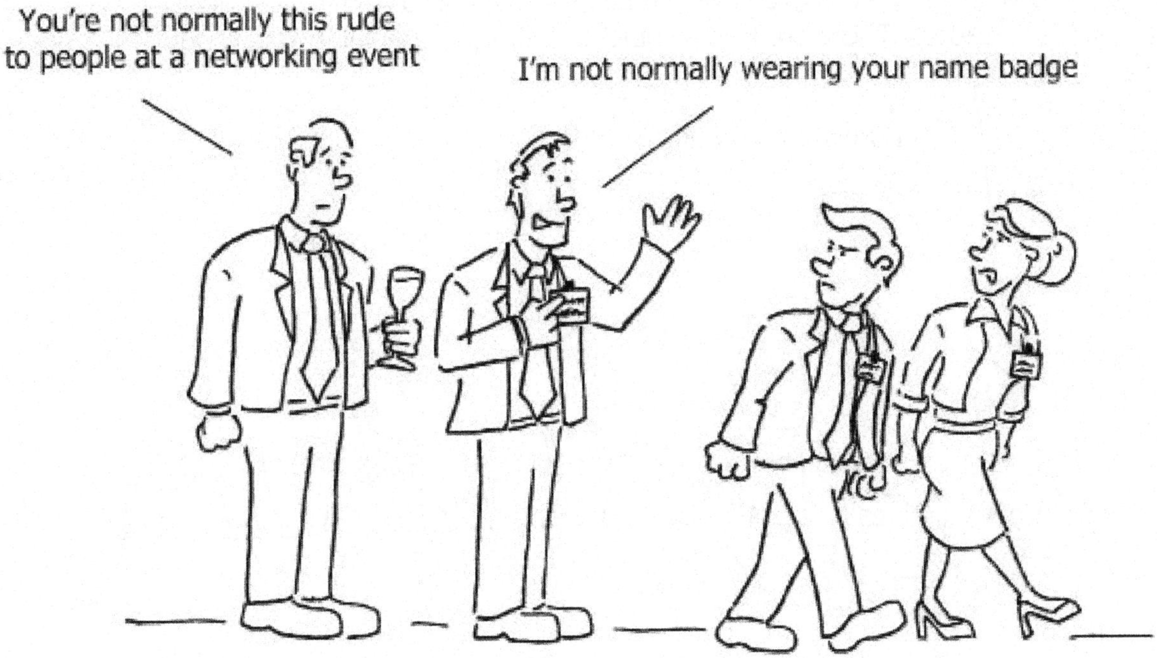
You're not normally this rude to people at a networking event
I'm not normally wearing your name badge

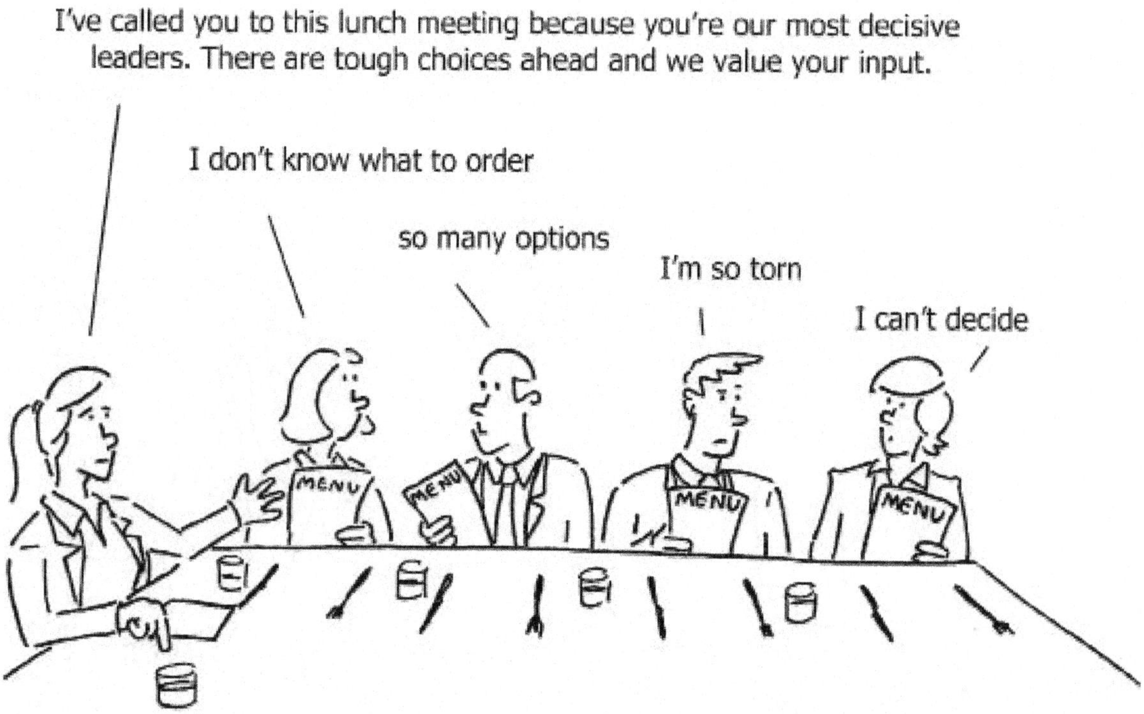
I've called you to this lunch meeting because you're our most decisive leaders. There are tough choices ahead and we value your input.
I don't know what to order
so many options
I'm so torn
I can't decide
MENU
MENU
MENU
MENU

Why are these guys making a deal in the office?

The boss said he wanted to see keeper-foreman syndicators

49

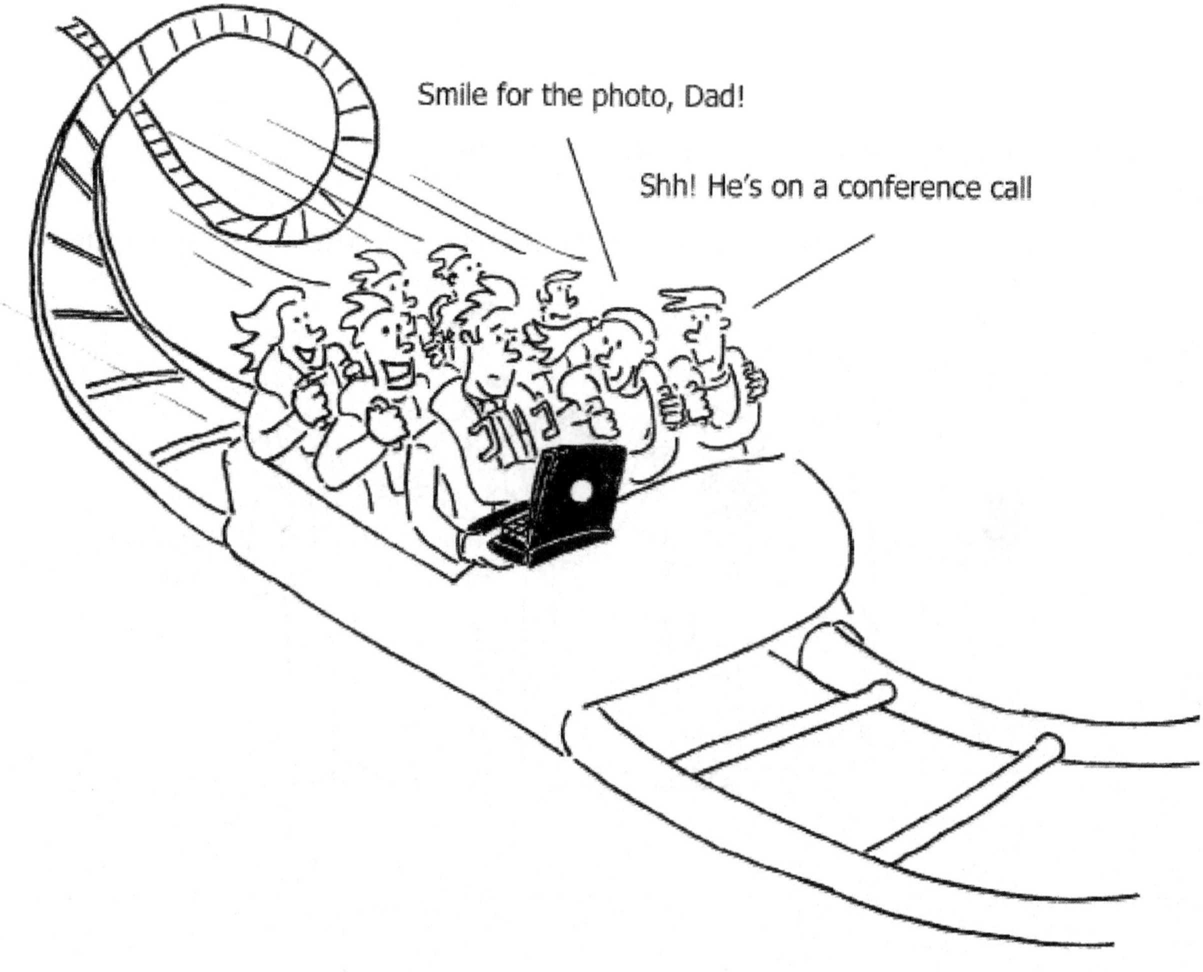
Smile for the photo, Dad!
Shh! He's on a conference call

Welcome to your one-to-one review.
Please take a seat...

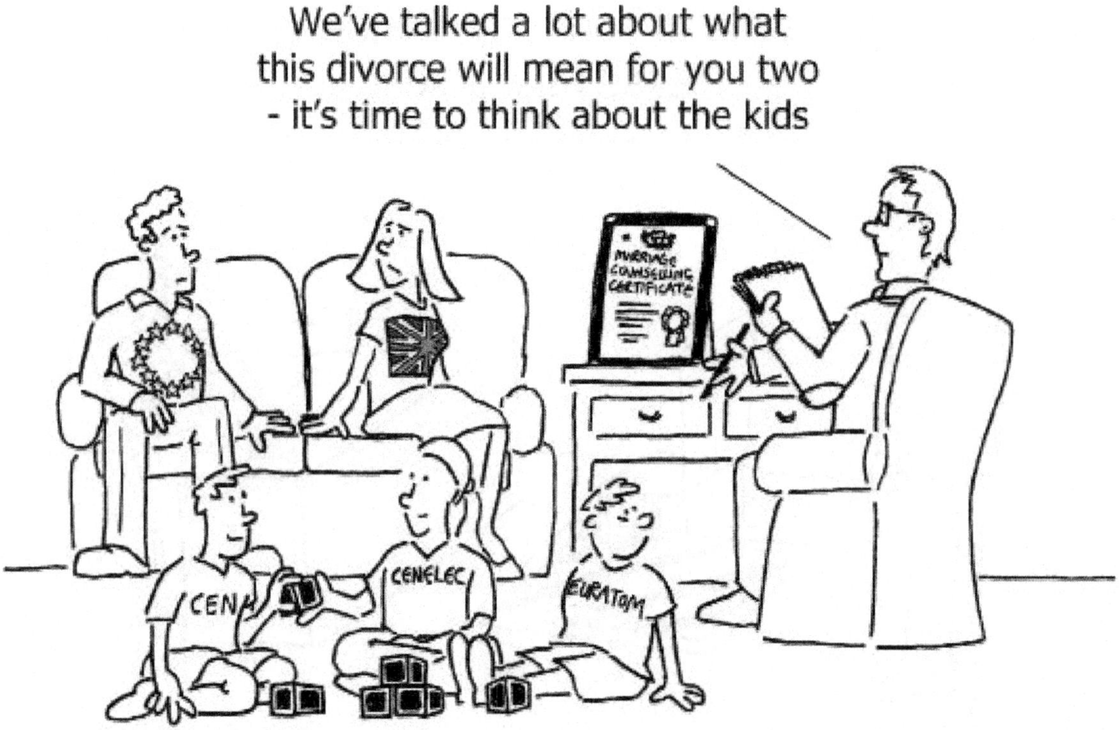
We've talked a lot about what this divorce will mean for you two - it's time to think about the kids
CEN
CENELEC
EURATOM

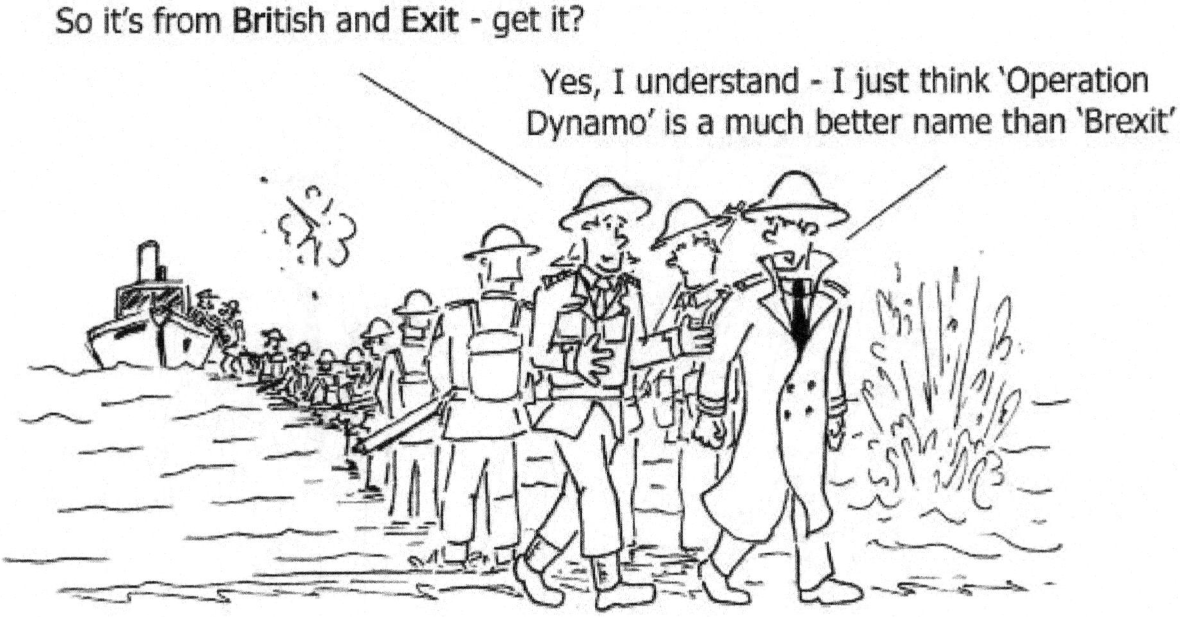
So it's from British and Exit - get it?
Yes, I understand - I just think 'Operation Dynamo' is a much better name than 'Brexit'

Perhaps they meant the clothes
inside the suit carrier?

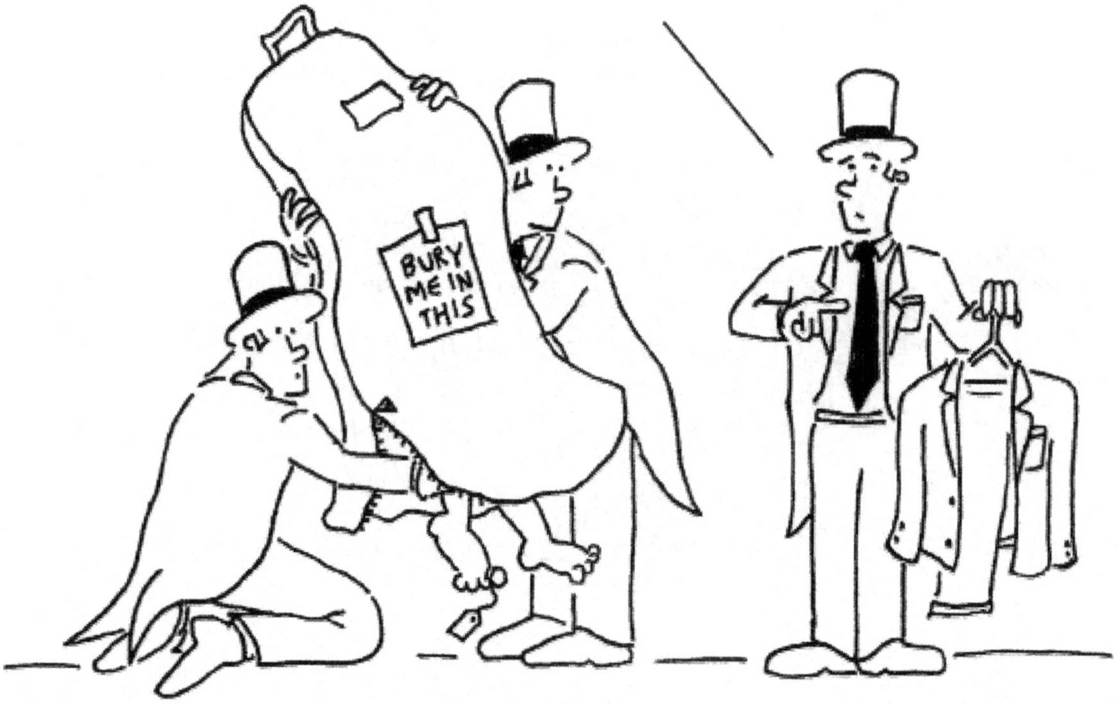
BURY ME IN THIS

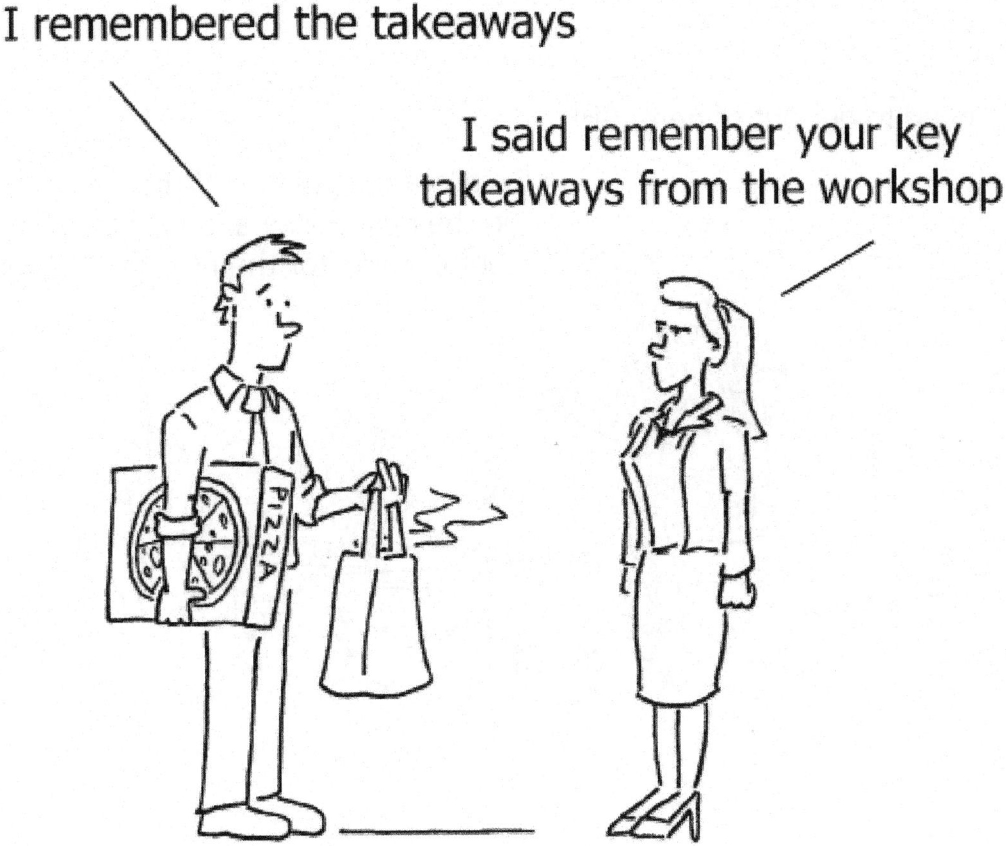
I remembered the takeaways
I said remember your key takeaways from the workshop
PIZZA

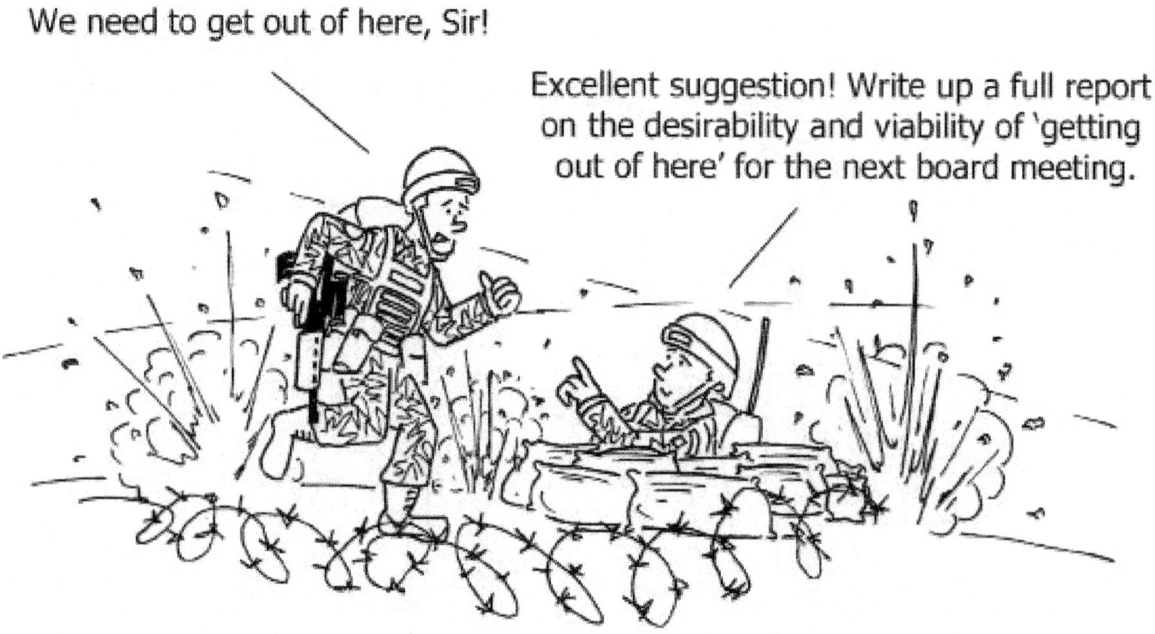
We need to get out of here, Sir!
Excellent suggestion! Write up a full report on the desirability and viability of 'getting out of here' for the next board meeting.

"And you tell me over and over and over again my friend..."*

World News

Alright, I'll admit that you could almost substitute US News for World News. A lot of material has been provided from that direction. Donald Trump has made a lot of headlines. The news cycle and the revolving door of the White House staff spin so fast that several cartoons have been abandoned as the situation changes before the ink is dry.

However, these are some of those that made it through in time. Such is the influence of the US that even the cartoons featuring other parts of the world such as North Korea and the Middle East are tied back to the same place.

America continues to fascinate, terrify and entertain.

*Barry McGuire

If you swear the oath on this pocket Bible
your hands should appear normal size

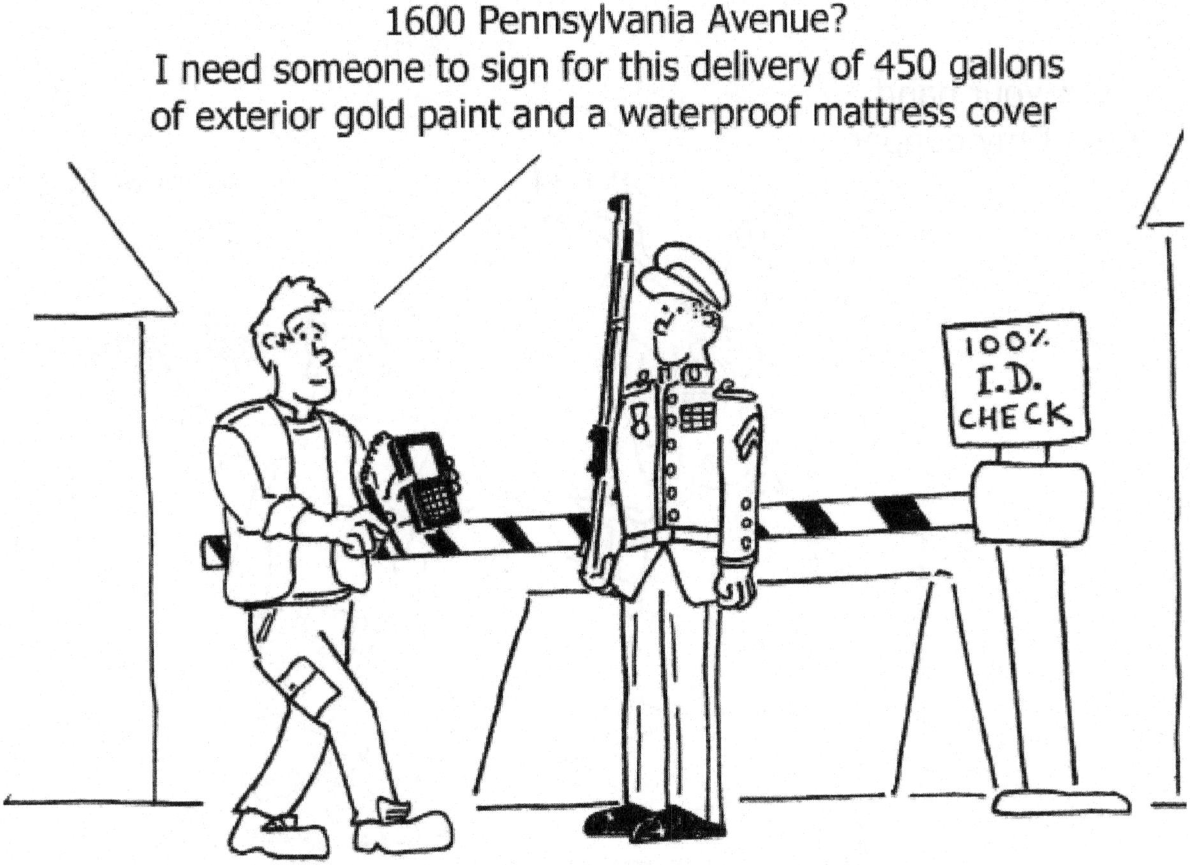
1600 Pennsylvania Avenue?
I need someone to sign for this delivery of 450 gallons of exterior gold paint and a waterproof mattress cover
100%
I.D.
CHECK

Day 1...

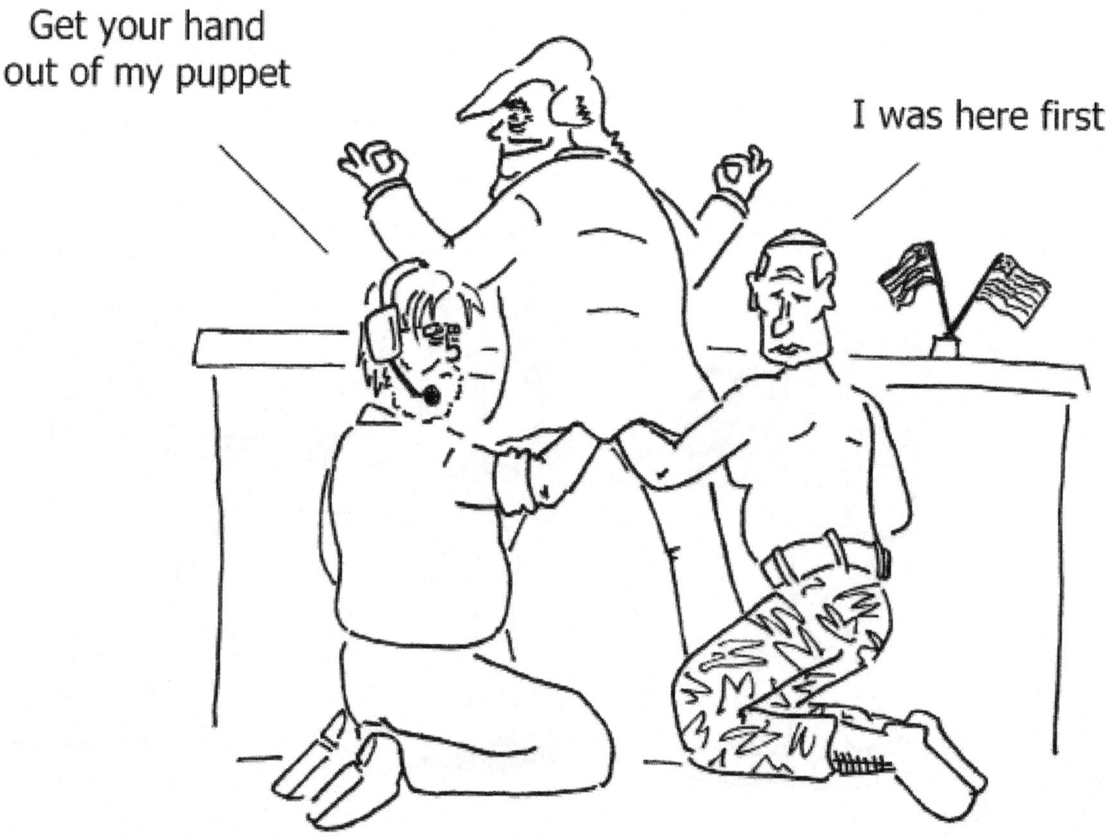
Get your hand out of my puppet
I was here first

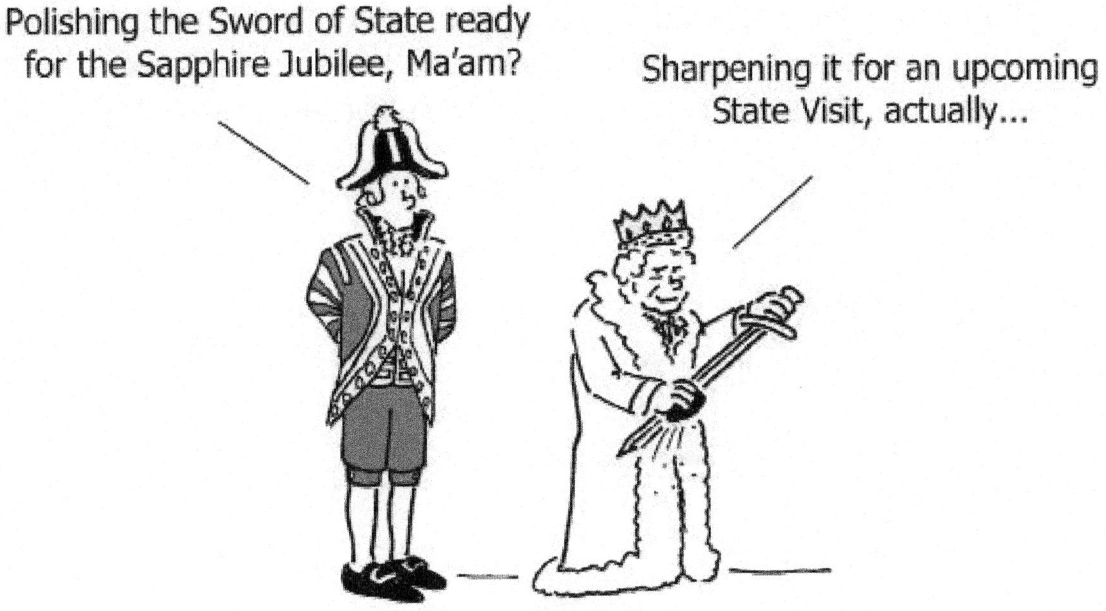
Polishing the Sword of State ready for the Sapphire Jubilee, Ma'am?
Sharpening it for an upcoming State Visit, actually...

You promised me a quiet, romantic Valentine's Dinner but all I can hear is that table next to us loudly discussing a classified strategic response to North Korean missile tests

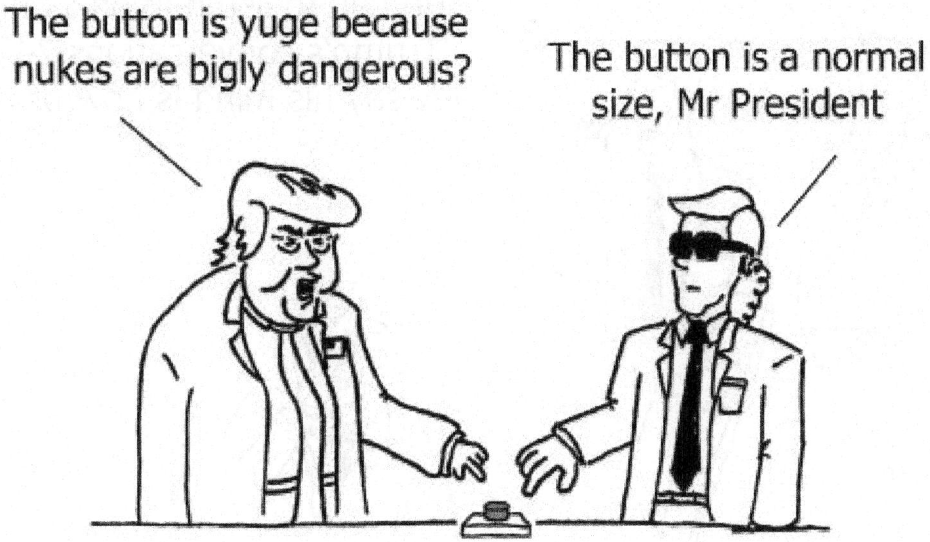
The button is yuge because nukes are bigly dangerous?
The button is a normal size, Mr President

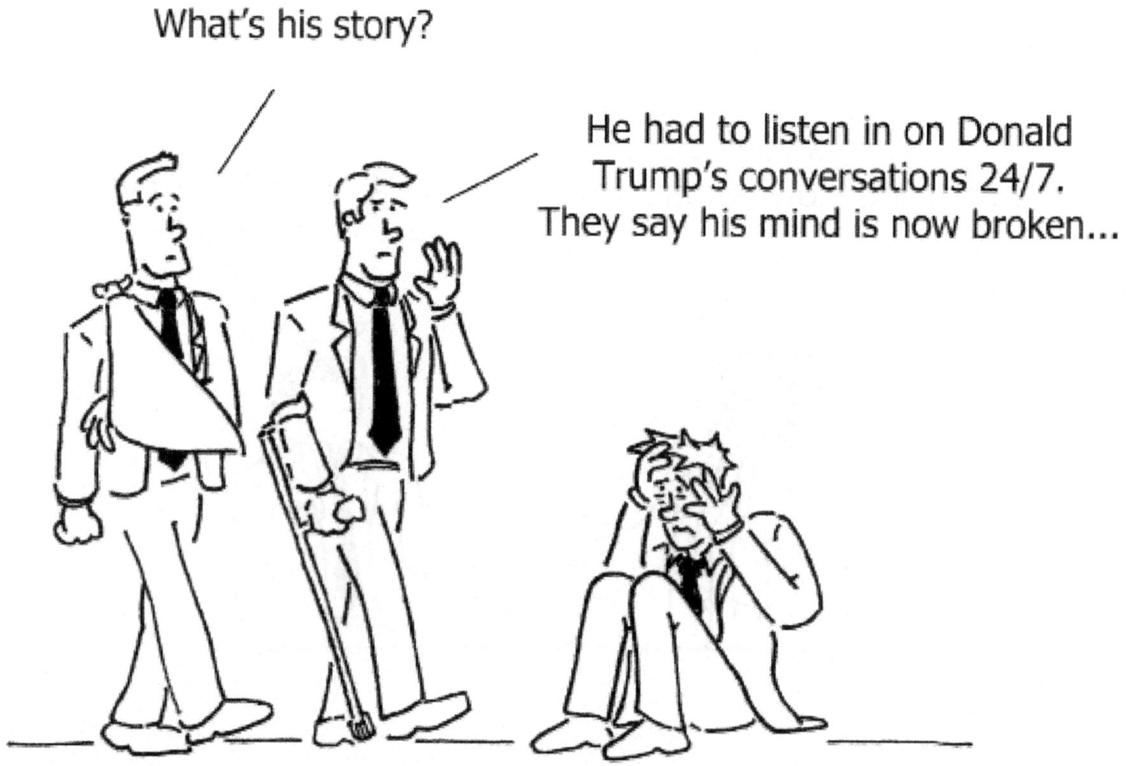
What's his story?
He had to listen in on Donald Trump's conversations 24/7. They say his mind is now broken...

FBI medical rehabilitation facility

Peacepsi

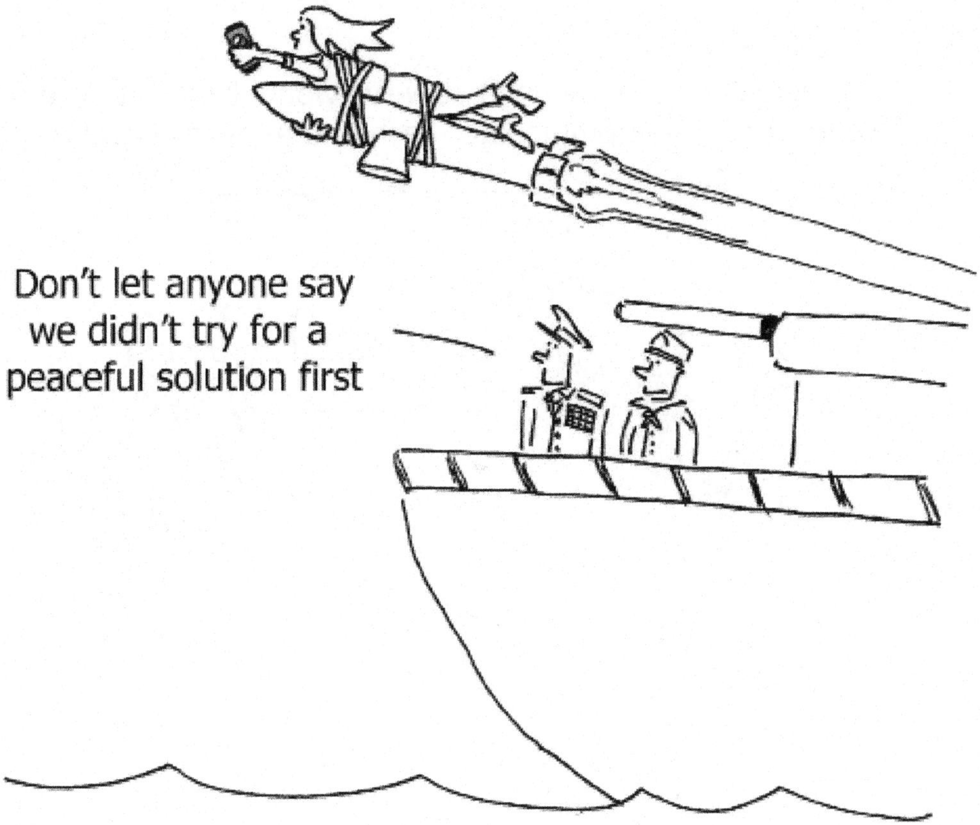
Don't let anyone say we didn't try for a peaceful solution first

Our stock may be plummeting but we've won a lucrative government contract to "re-accommodate" Bashar al-Assad from Damascus

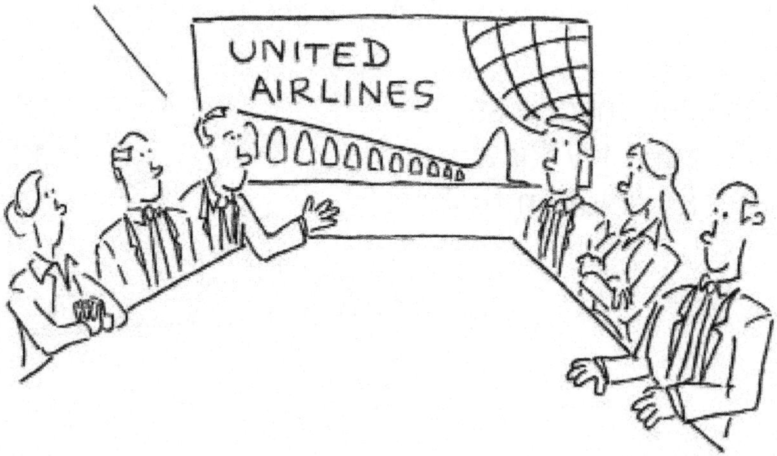
UNITED
AIRLINES

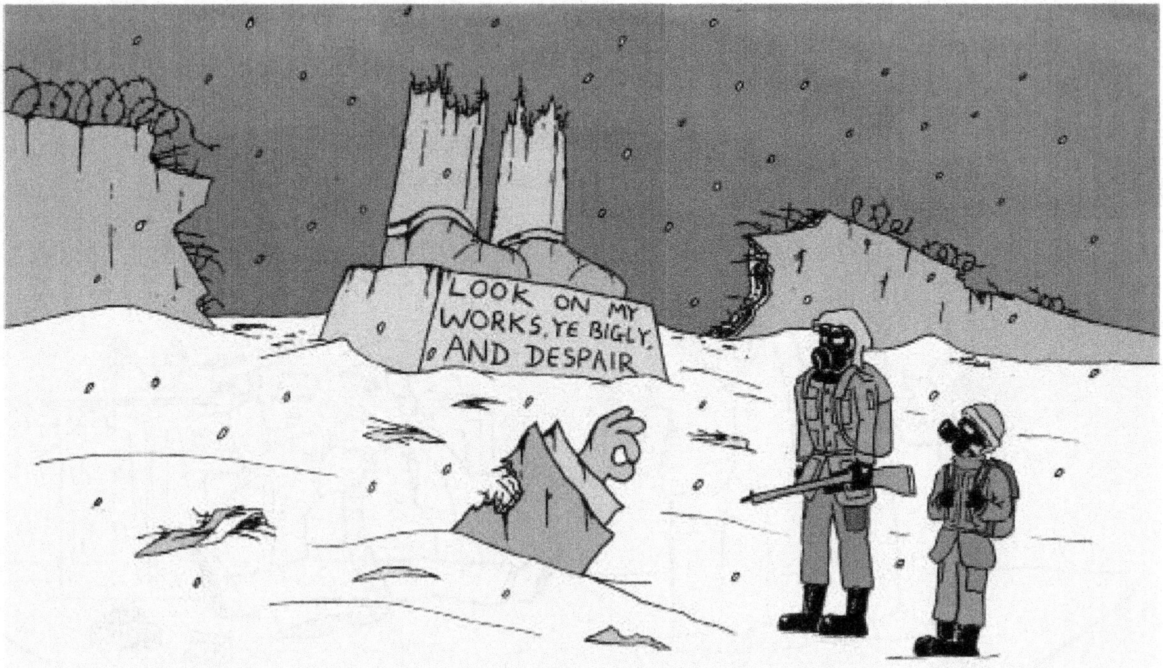
LOOK ON MY WORKS, YE BIGLY, AND DESPAIR

Dad, was this guy a jerk?

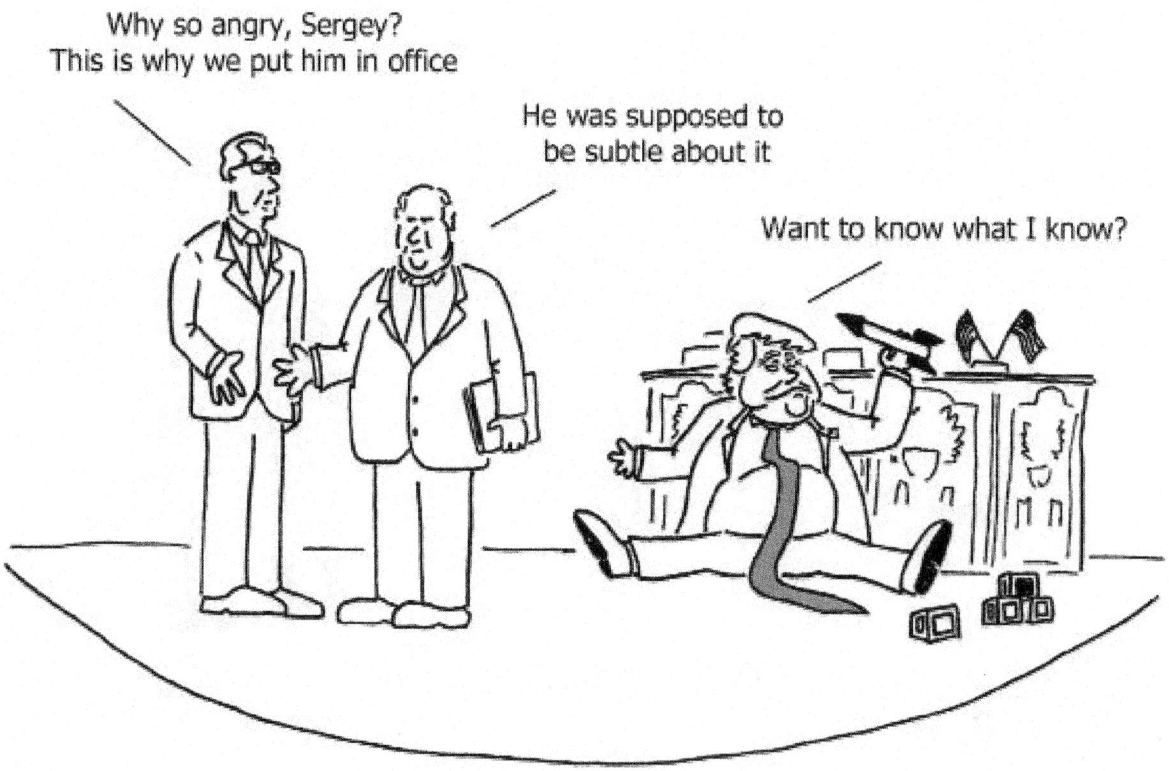
Why so angry, Sergey?
This is why we put him in office
He was supposed to
be subtle about it
Want to know what I know?

"We will not go quietly into the night! We wil not vanish without a fight!
When I get back from my golf game I'll share a gif of me punching an alien,
tweet about 'low-resource ETs', or just dismiss this whole invasion as FAKE NEWS!"

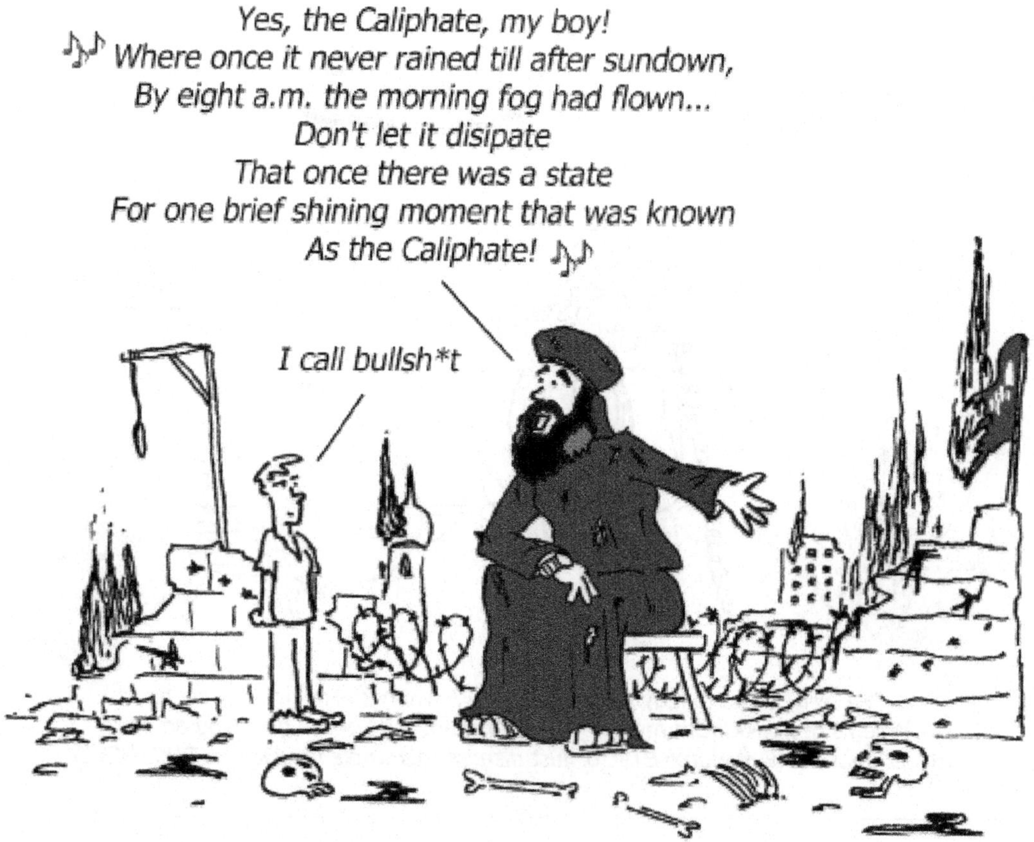
Yes, the Caliphate, my boy!
♪♪ Where once it never rained till after sundown,
By eight a.m. the morning fog had flown...
Don't let it disipate
That once there was a state
For one brief shining moment that was known
As the Caliphate! ♪♪
I call bullsh*t

InContinental Ballistic Missile

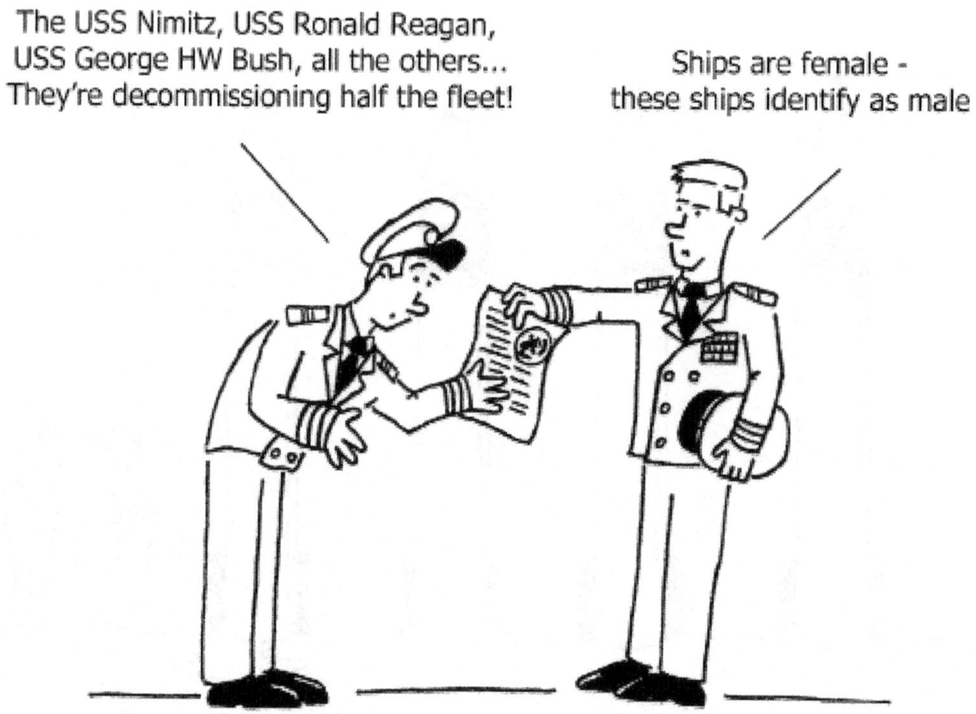
The USS Nimitz, USS Ronald Reagan, USS George HW Bush, all the others... They're decommissioning half the fleet!
Ships are female - these ships identify as male

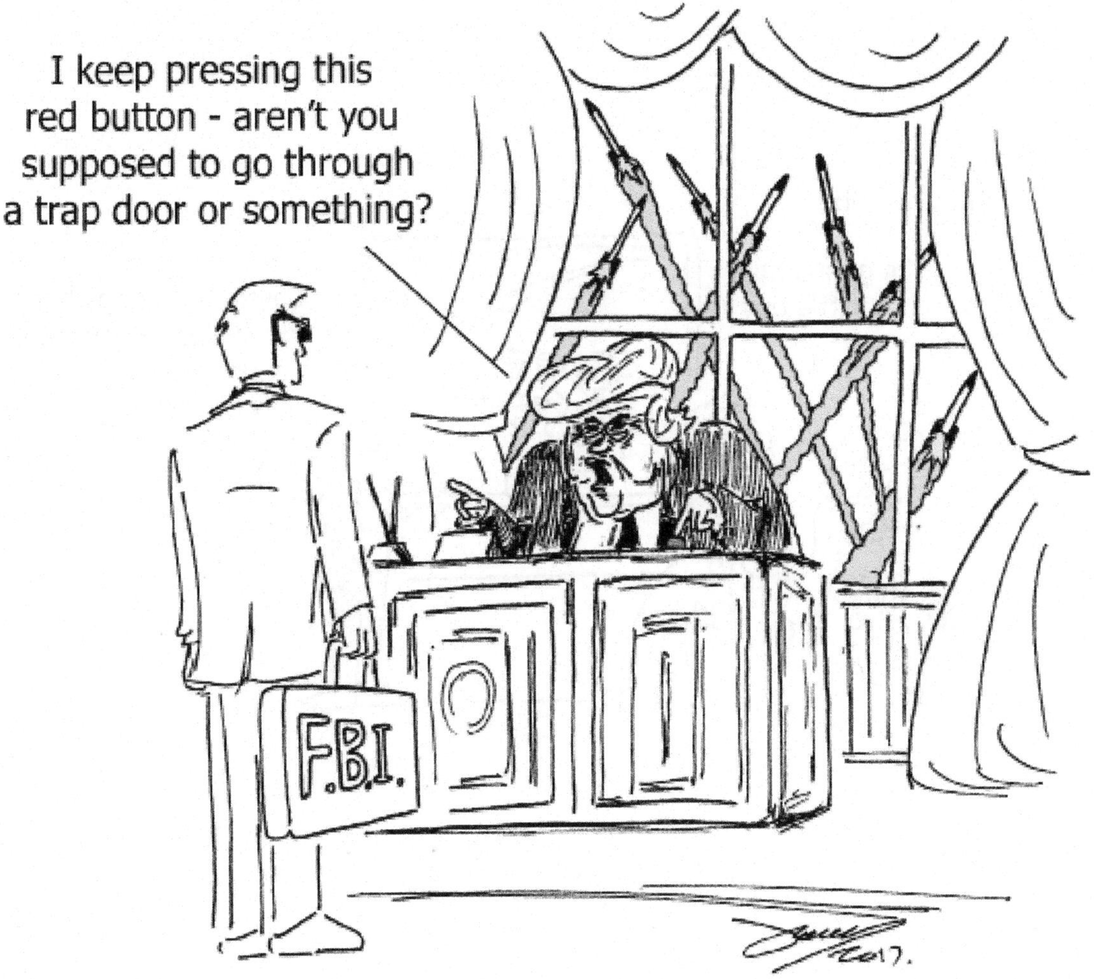
I keep pressing this red button - aren't you supposed to go through a trap door or something?
F.B.I.

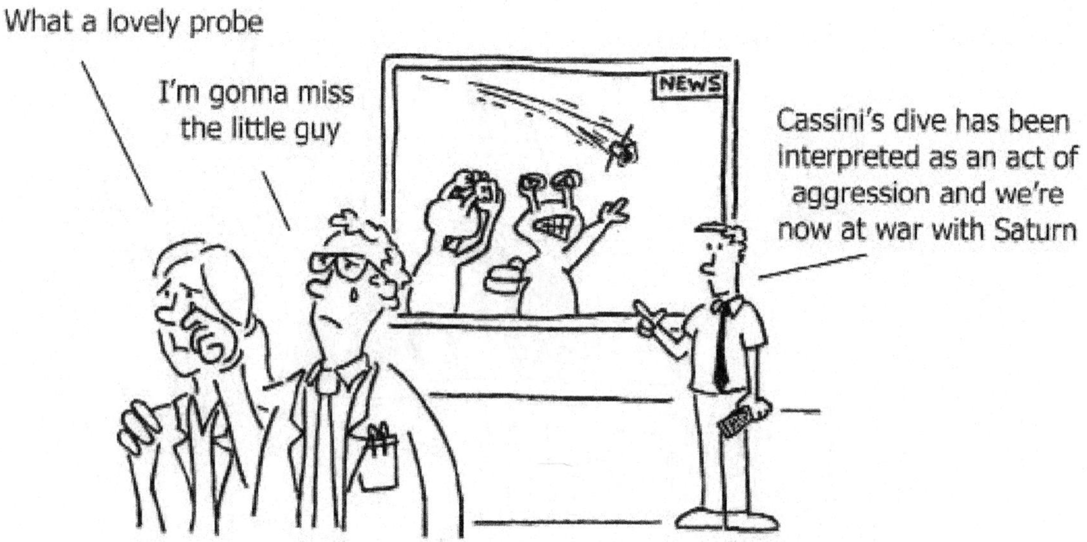
What a lovely probe
I'm gonna miss the little guy
NEWS
Cassini's dive has been interpreted as an act of aggression and we're now at war with Saturn

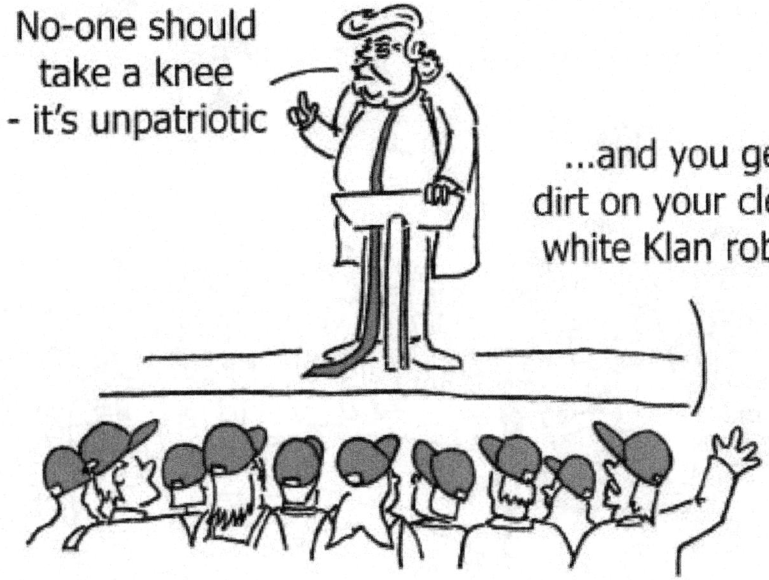
No-one should
take a knee
- it's unpatriotic
...and you get
dirt on your clean
white Klan robes

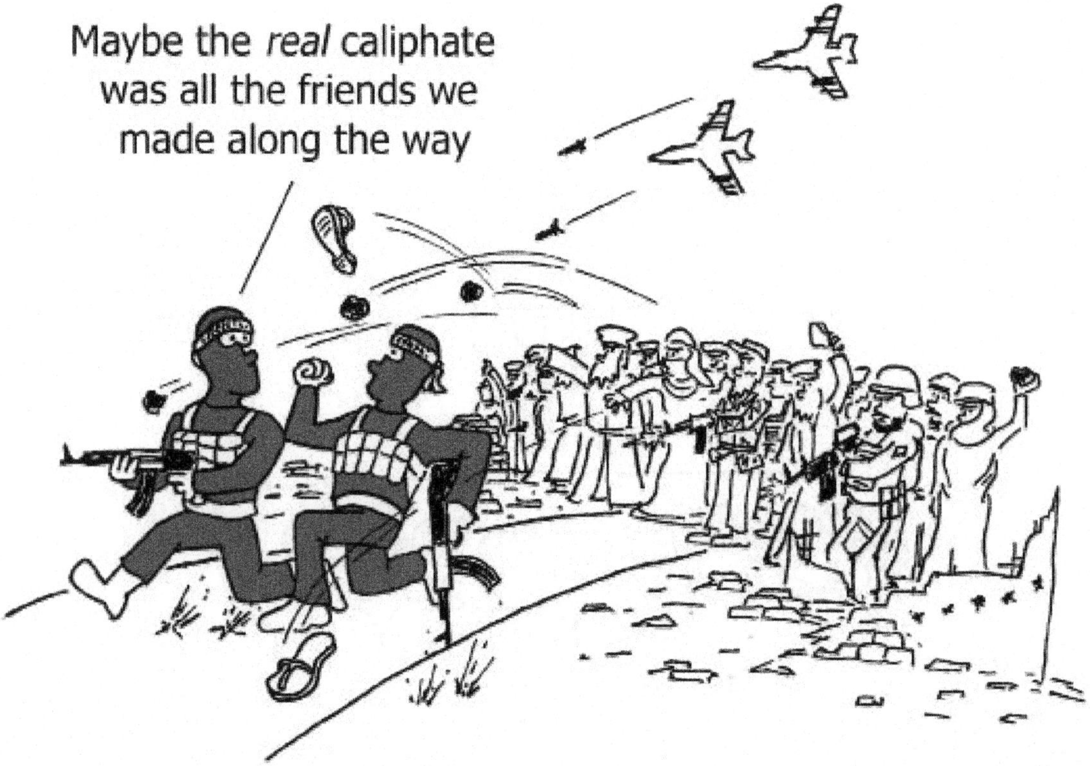
Maybe the *real* caliphate
was all the friends we
made along the way

Here be dragons (and sometimes robots)

Entertainment and Culture

In a world of raised threat levels and nuclear anxiety, entertainment isn't so much luxury but feels more like therapy. It's a chance to forget about real life terrors for a while and focus on fictional terrors instead.

Perhaps we're doing it wrong.

This chapter does indeed provide a cartoon commentary on some of the (make believe) events from Westeros and Gilead but also deals with some real world cultural issues.

Expect to find cartoons featuring some of this country's most significant cultural establishments, including the Natural History Museum, the Six Nations Championship and the Great Yarmouth Sealife Centre.

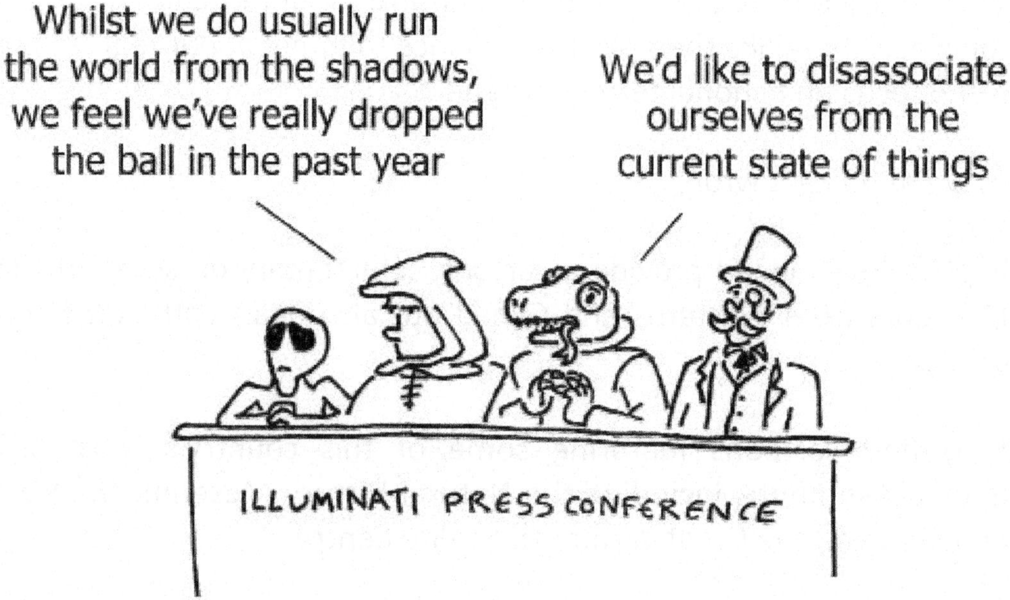
Whilst we do usually run the world from the shadows, we feel we've really dropped the ball in the past year
We'd like to disassociate ourselves from the current state of things
ILLUMINATI PRESS CONFERENCE

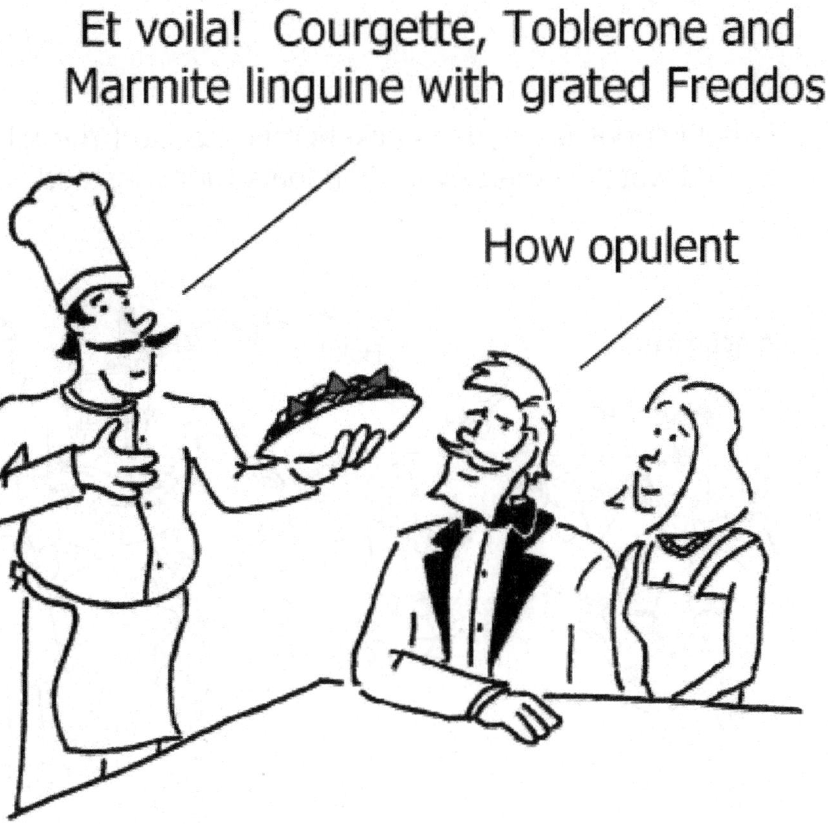
Et voila! Courgette, Toblerone and Marmite linguine with grated Freddos
How opulent

Extravagance in 2017

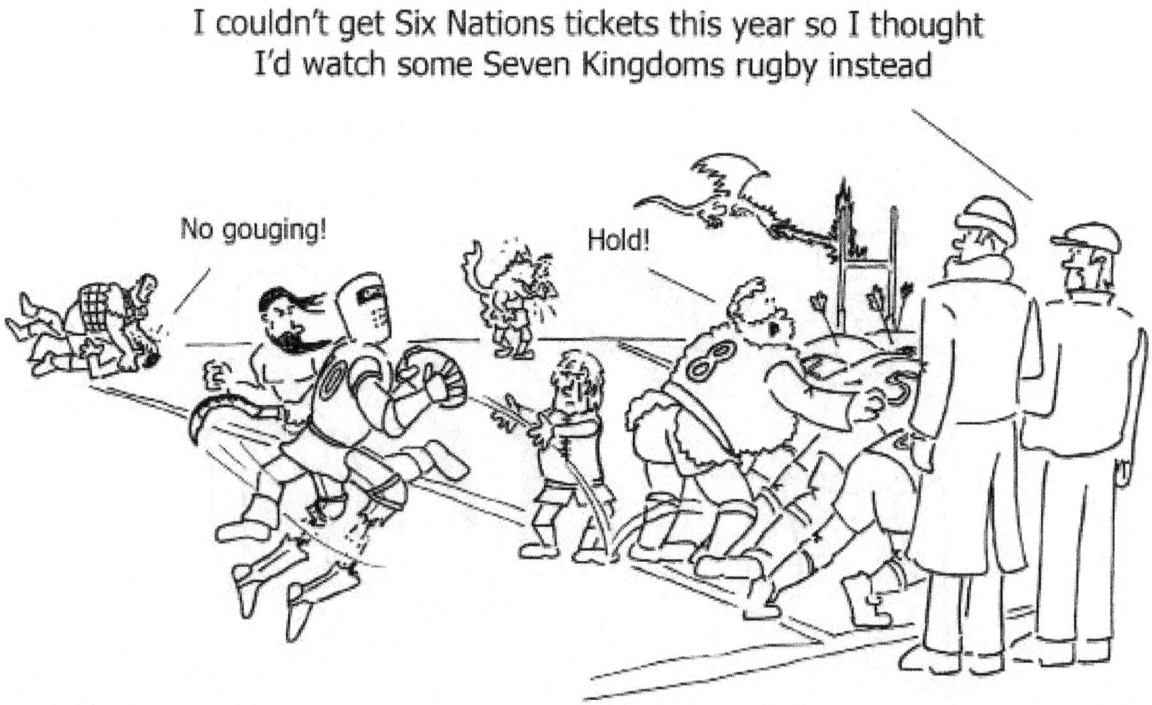
I couldn't get Six Nations tickets this year so I thought
I'd watch some Seven Kingdoms rugby instead
No gouging!
Hold!

Now, you'll hear some chefs say to use goose fat but I always layer the roasting tin with freshly minted five pound notes

We were going to travel here to share our advanced technology and perpetual energy, but we heard about travel bans and deporting aliens.

So...jog on around your little sun, Mankind.

NASA Press Conference

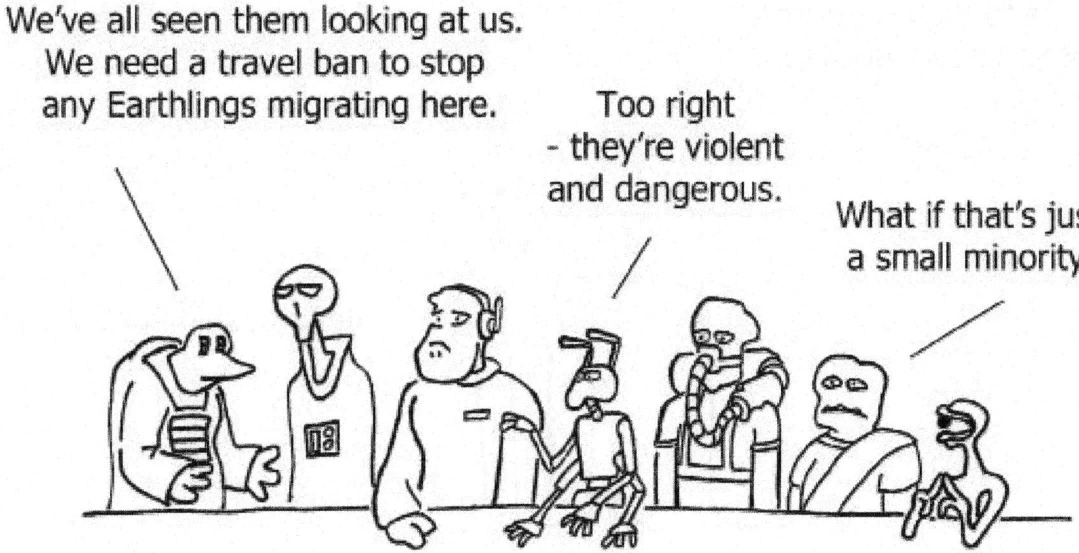
We've all seen them looking at us. We need a travel ban to stop any Earthlings migrating here.
Too right - they're violent and dangerous.
What if that's just a small minority?

TRAPPIST-1
UNITED COUNCIL OF PLANETS

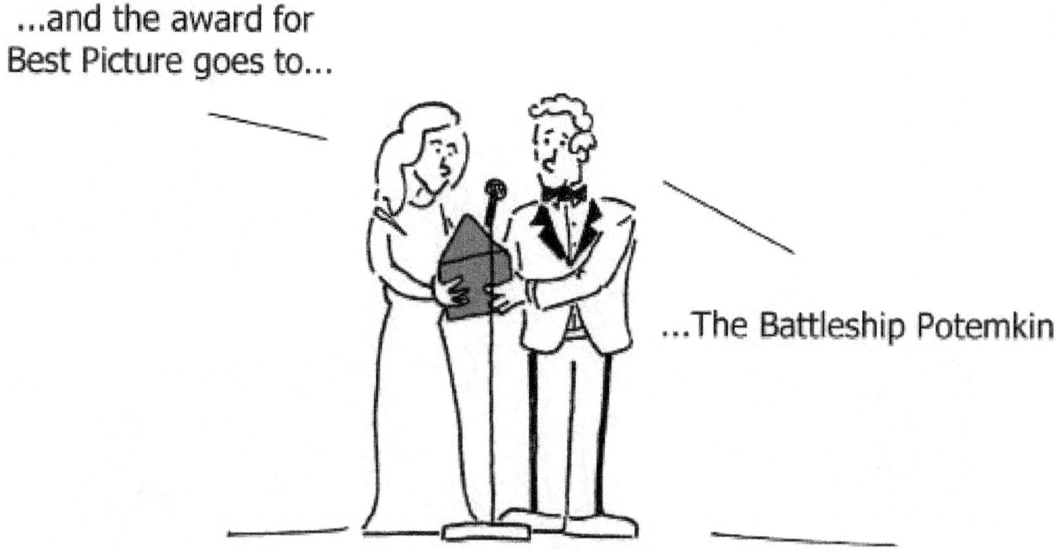
...and the award for
Best Picture goes to...
...The Battleship Potemkin

Allegations that Russian hackers influenced the Academy Awards

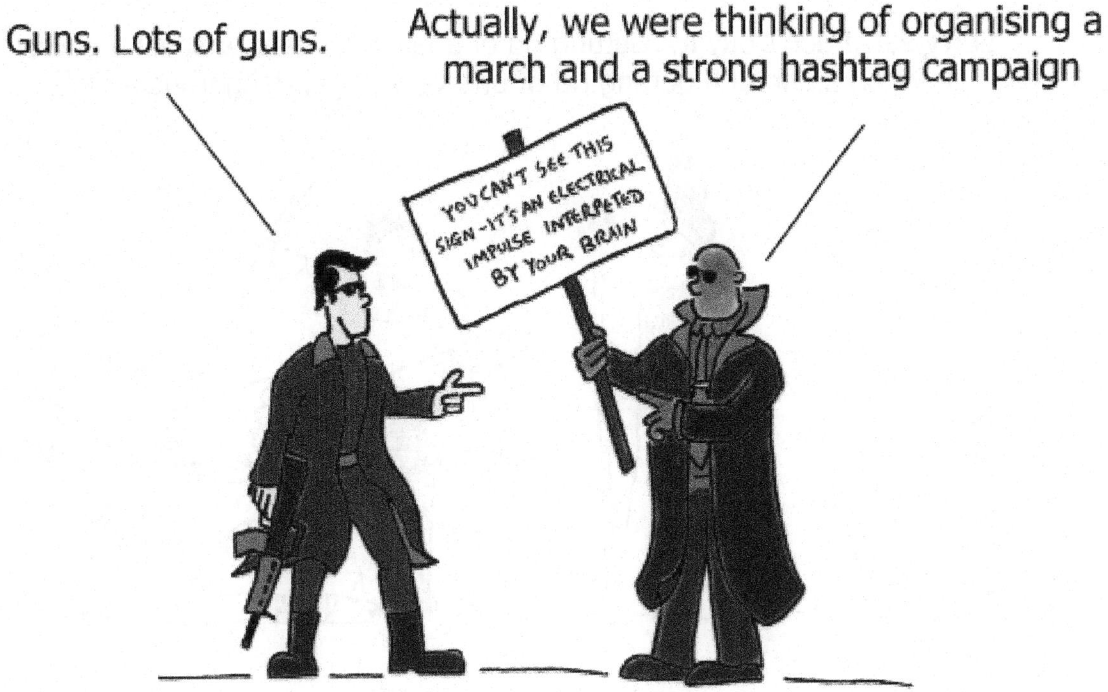
Guns. Lots of guns.
Actually, we were thinking of organising a march and a strong hashtag campaign
YOU CAN'T SEE THIS SIGN - IT'S AN ELECTRICAL IMPULSE INTERPRETED BY YOUR BRAIN

The Matrix - rebooted for the 21st century

Sorry Pat, I don't buy it. Getting rid of a large number of small reptiles is not on a par with getting rid of one very large, dangerous repltile

Saintly pest control

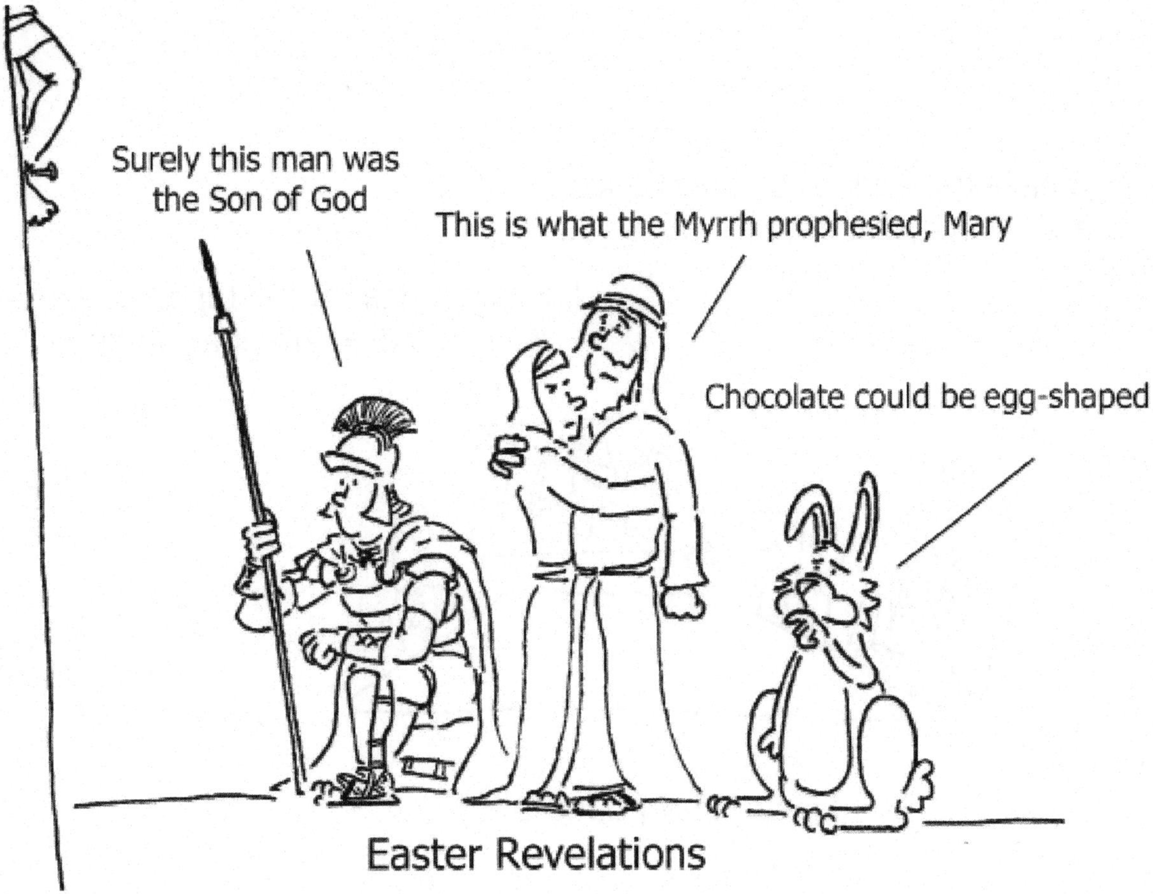
Surely this man was the Son of God
This is what the Myrrh prophesied, Mary
Chocolate could be egg-shaped

Easter Revelations

You have the right to be questioned by a pupil one school-year above you
For the benefit of the tape, we are viewing a diagram of a 'wedgie'

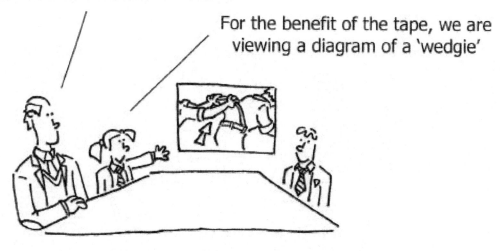

Line of Playground Duty

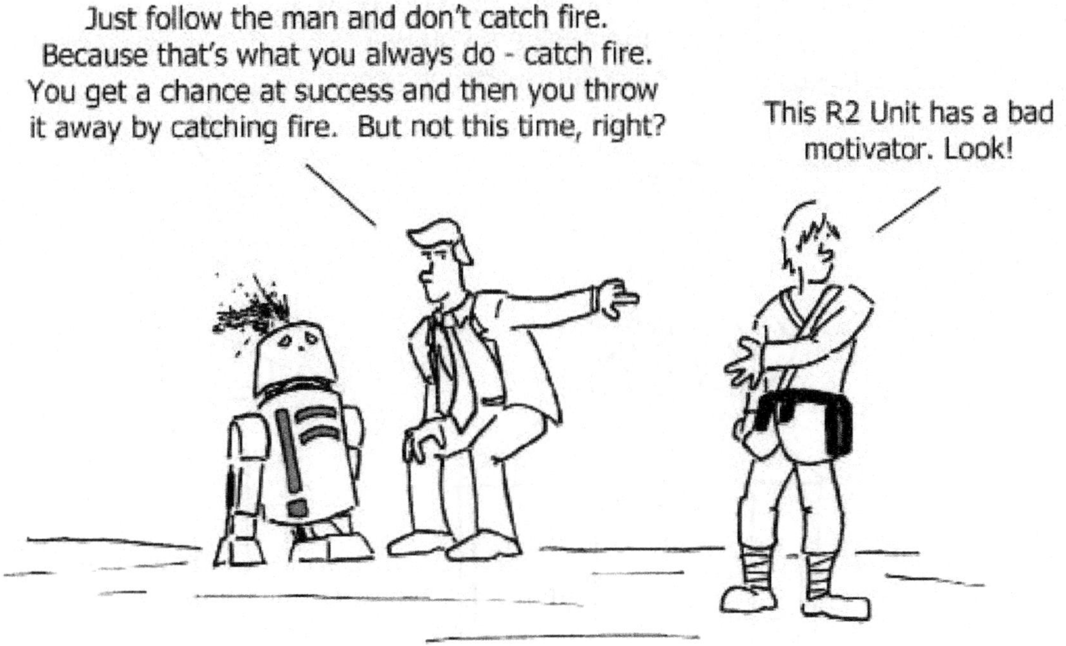
Just follow the man and don't catch fire. Because that's what you always do - catch fire. You get a chance at success and then you throw it away by catching fire. But not this time, right?
This R2 Unit has a bad motivator. Look!

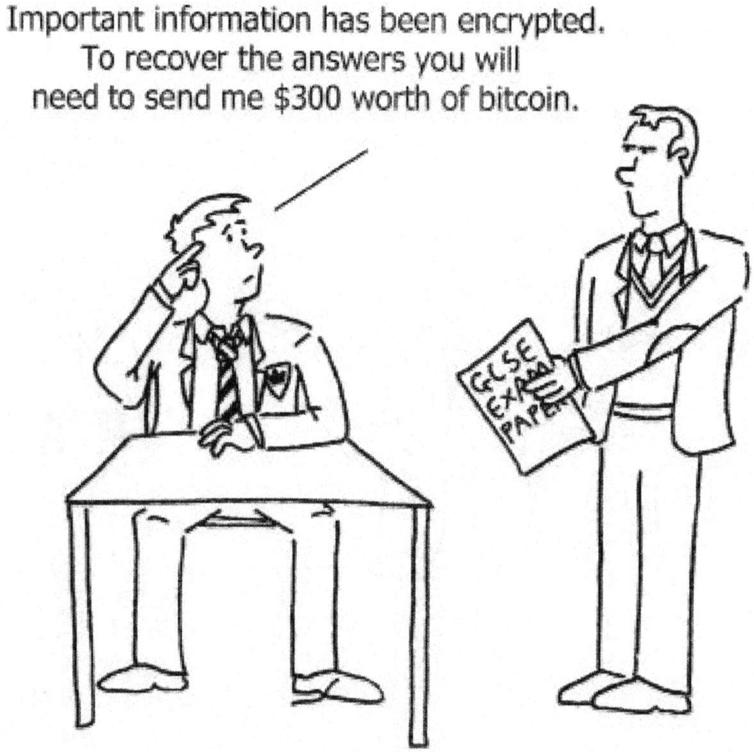
Important information has been encrypted. To recover the answers you will need to send me $300 worth of bitcoin.
GCSE

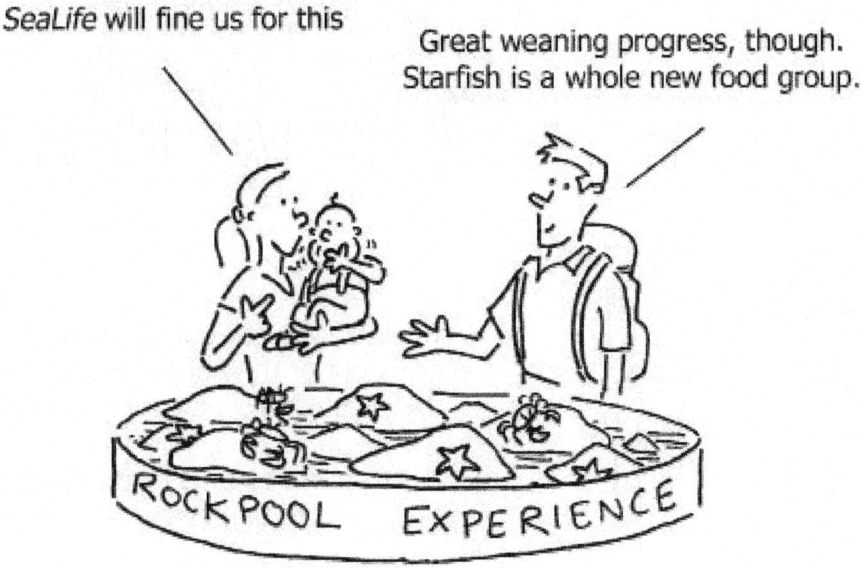
SeaLife will fine us for this
Great weaning progress, though.
Starfish is a whole new food group.
ROCKPOOL EXPERIENCE

I know you wanted our office to emulate the grandeur or the Natural History Museum but I couldn't source a blue whale...

Jeff from accounts is the largest creature on payroll, though.

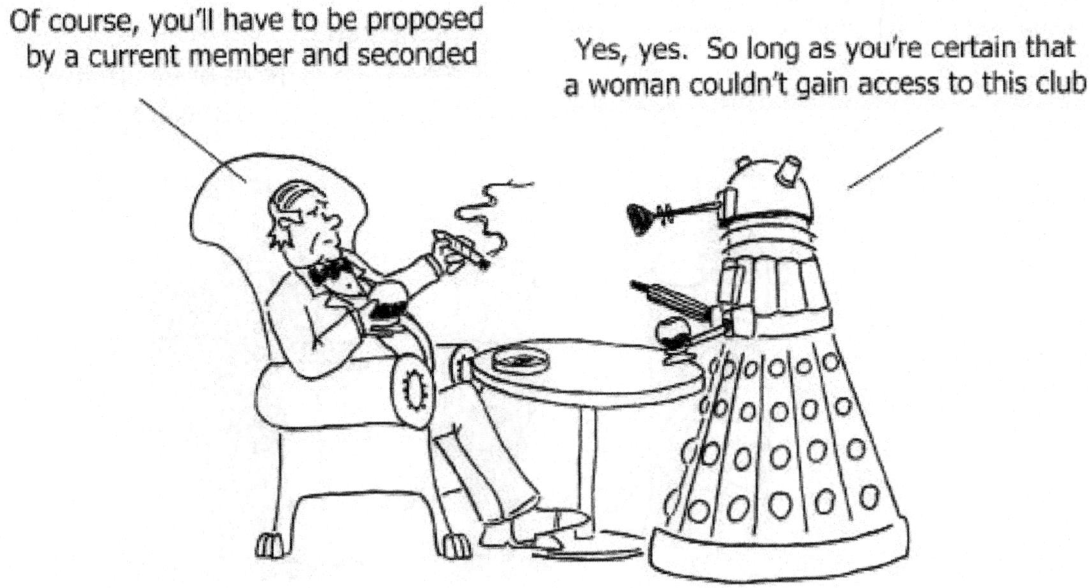
Of course, you'll have to be proposed by a current member and seconded
Yes, yes. So long as you're certain that a woman couldn't gain access to this club

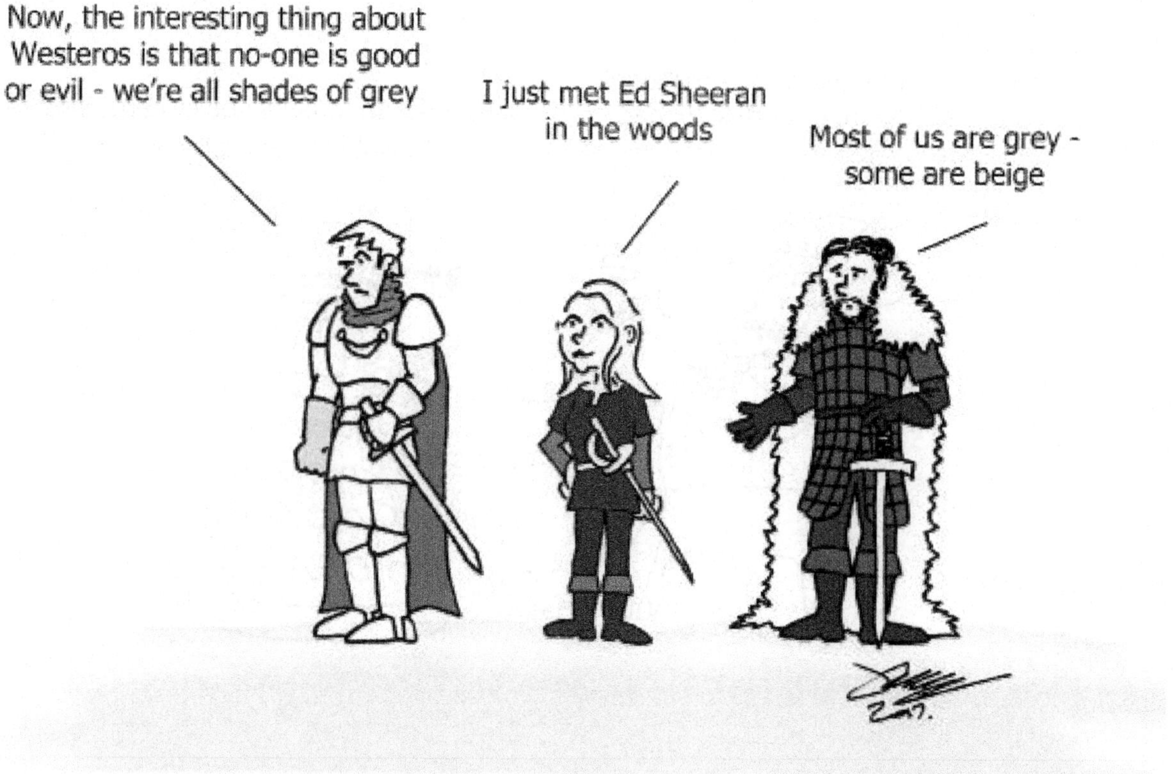
Now, the interesting thing about Westeros is that no-one is good or evil - we're all shades of grey
I just met Ed Sheeran in the woods
Most of us are grey - some are beige

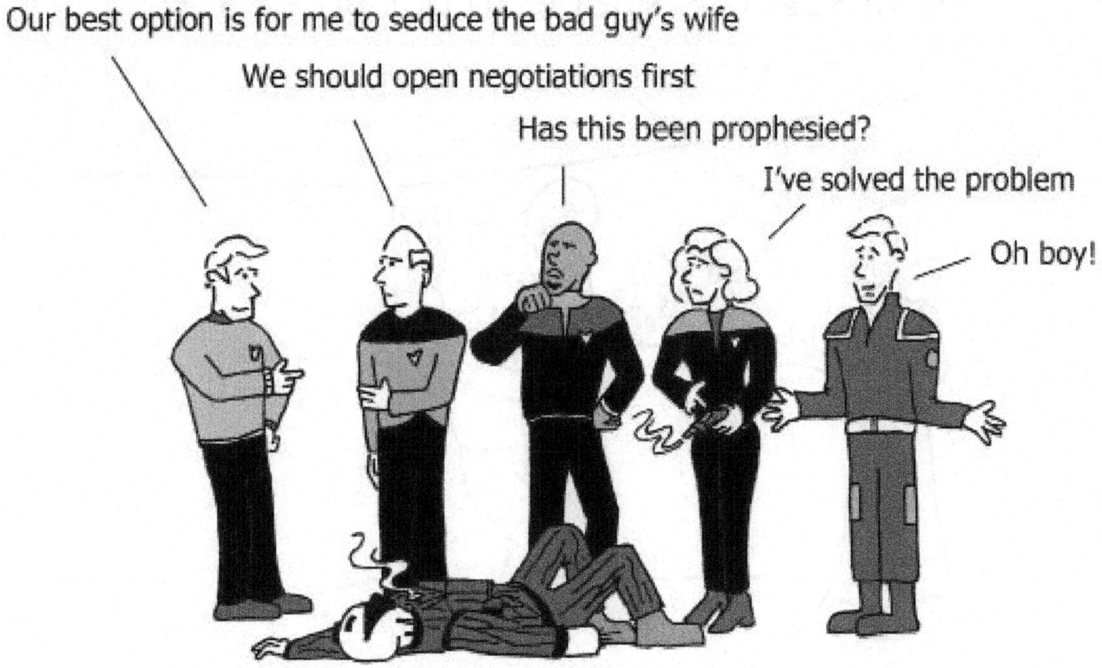
Our best option is for me to seduce the bad guy's wife
We should open negotiations first
Has this been prophesied?
I've solved the problem
Oh boy!

Star Trek Captains

My husband is unable to put up shelves

The Handyman's Tale

It's coming straight for us!
What are you doing back there?
MARSHMALLOWS

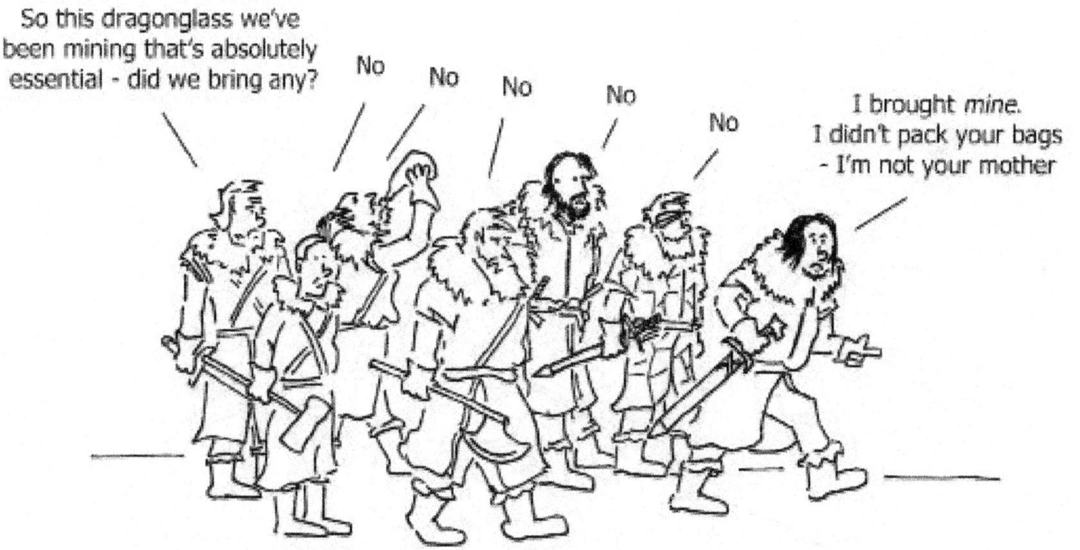
So this dragonglass we've been mining that's absolutely essential - did we bring any?
No
No
No
No
No
I brought *mine*. I didn't pack your bags - I'm not your mother

Jon Snow's Less-Than-Magnificent Seven

"First as tragedy, second as farce"*

History

There is no specific reason that a review of 2017 should feature a chapter on History other than it is my passion. I believe it is an incredibly valuable discipline and that it can also provide a lot of enjoyment. I think many people share this passion and I believe many more should.

The events cartooned here didn't occur in 2017, but they were either celebrated or commemorated at a particular point this year or proved to be particularly insightful and relevant to modern day happenings. Some are featured because a specific anniversary gives them special poignancy this year.

The Battle of Waterloo is featured because I had an idea about a chicken that I thought was funny.

*Karl Marx

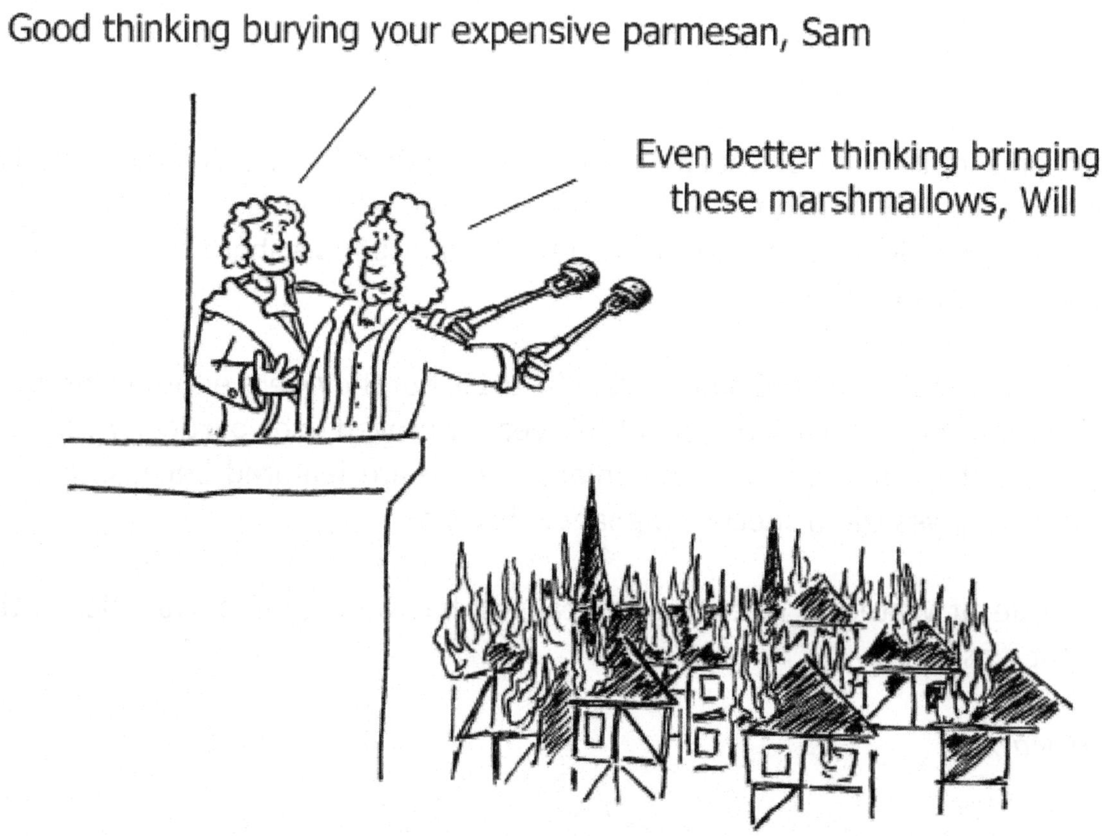
Good thinking burying your expensive parmesan, Sam
Even better thinking bringing these marshmallows, Will

Admiral Penn and Samuel Pepys watch The Great Fire from All Hallows' tower

Why don't we eat the penguins, Ernest?
My hands are too cold to get the wrappers off

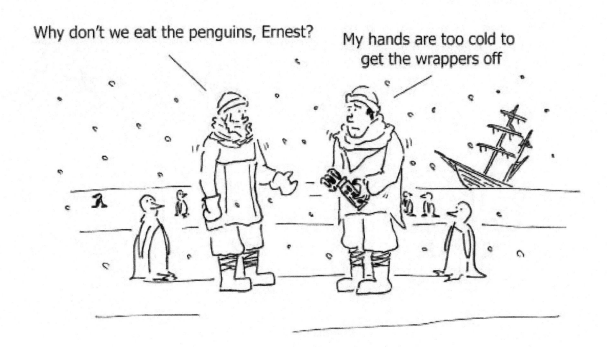

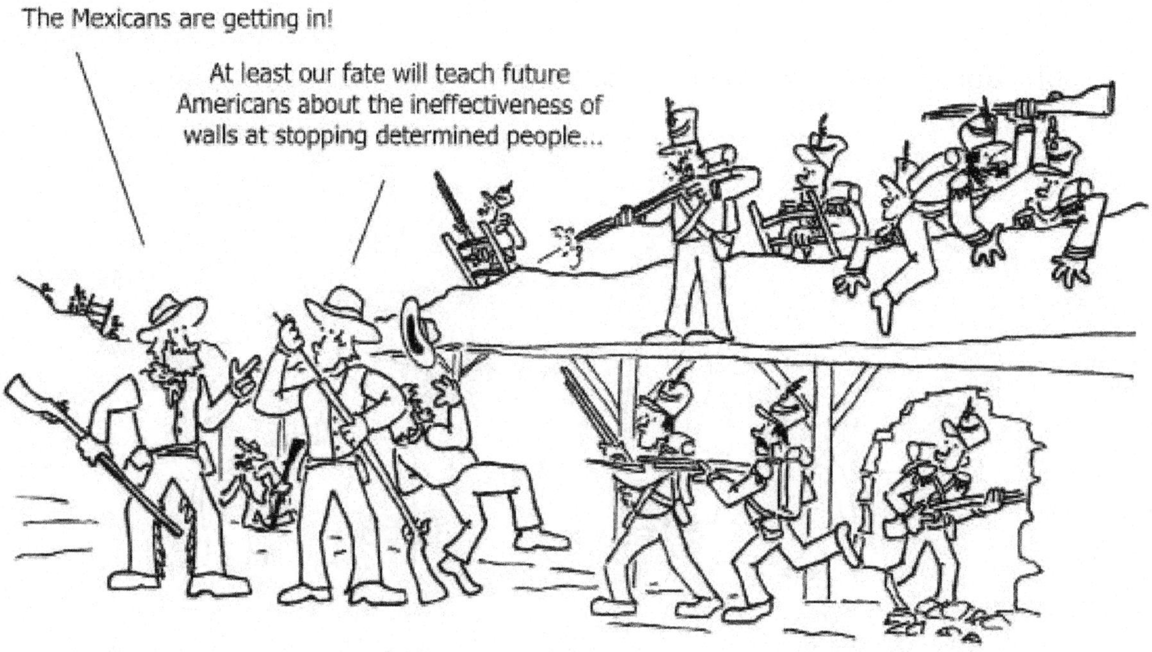
The Mexicans are getting in!
At least our fate will teach future Americans about the ineffectiveness of walls at stopping determined people...

The Alamo 1836

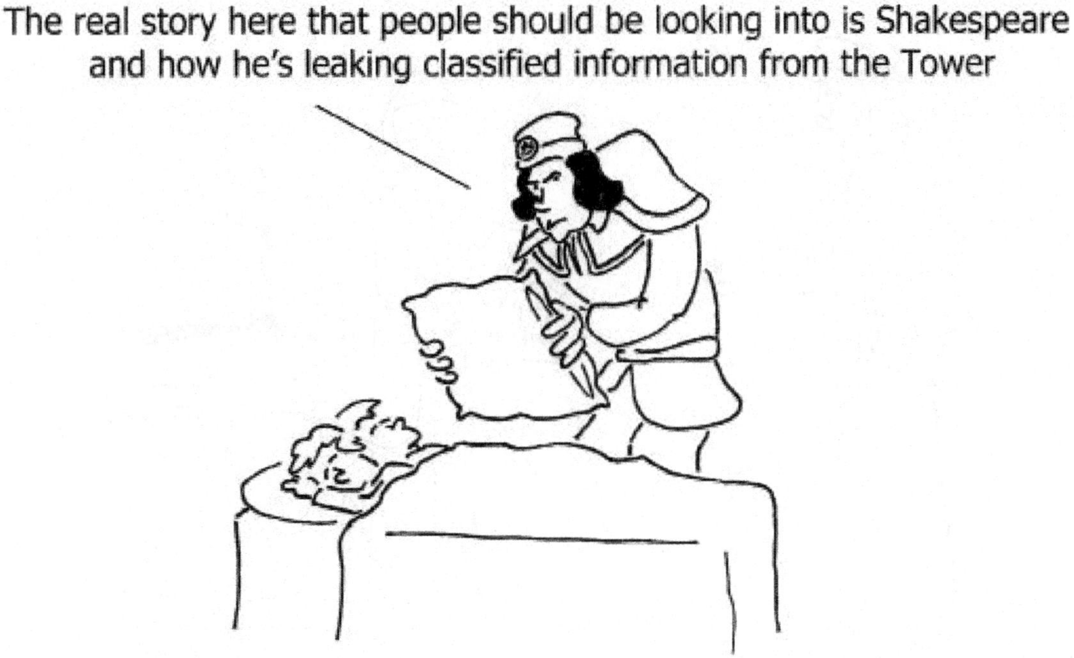
The real story here that people should be looking into is Shakespeare and how he's leaking classified information from the Tower

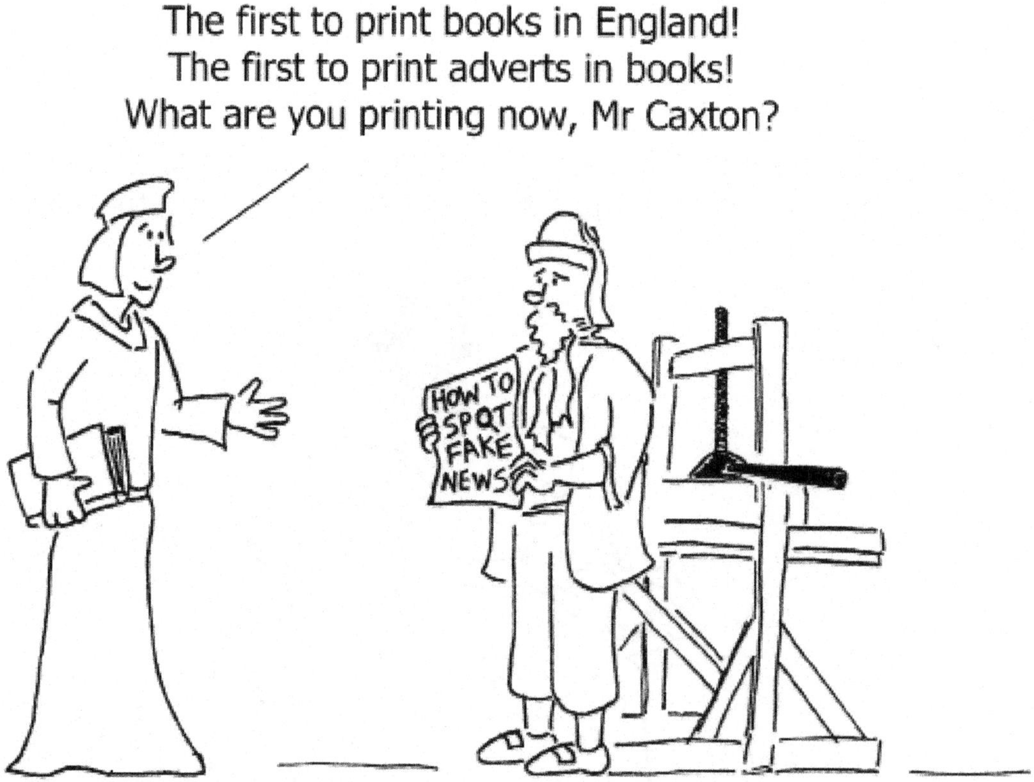
The first to print books in England!
The first to print adverts in books!
What are you printing now, Mr Caxton?
HOW TO SPOT FAKE NEWS

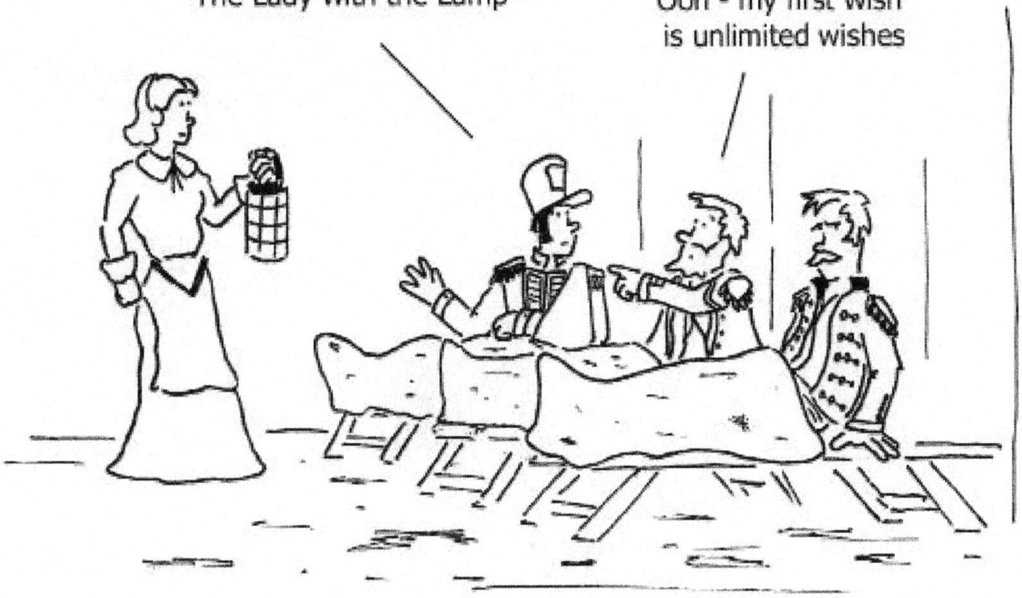
It's Florence Nightingale,
'The Lady with the Lamp'
Ooh - my first wish
is unlimited wishes

Scutari 1854

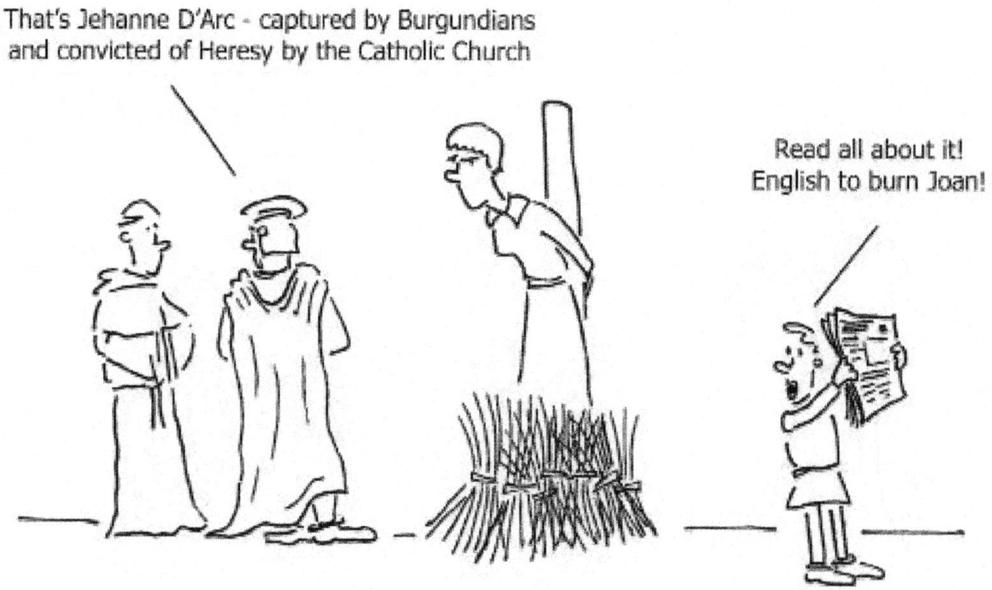
That's Jehanne D'Arc - captured by Burgundians and convicted of Heresy by the Catholic Church
Read all about it! English to burn Joan!

Fake News 1431

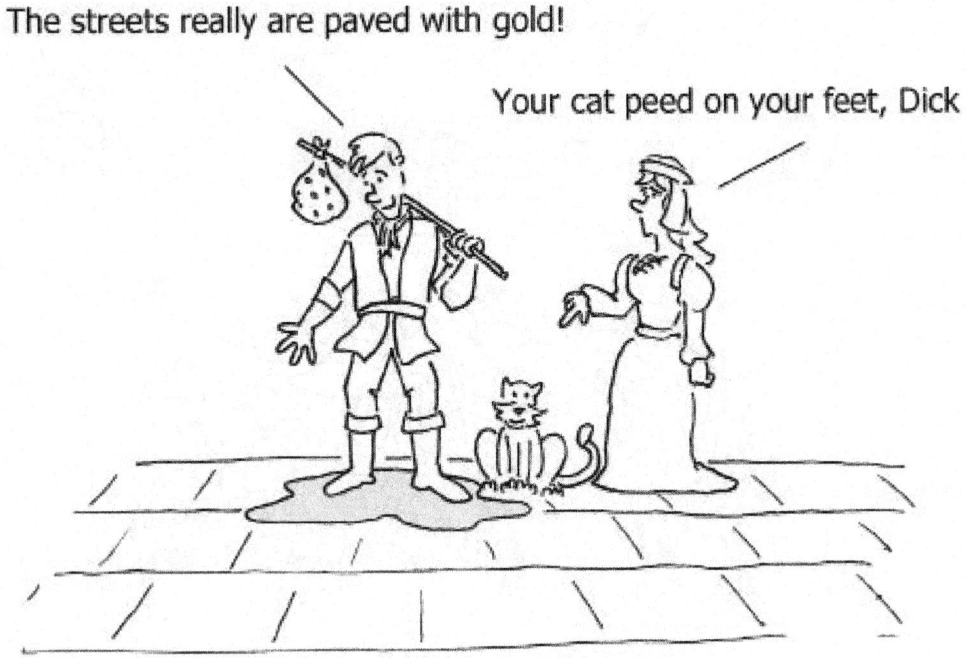
The streets really are paved with gold!
Your cat peed on your feet, Dick

Sir Richard Whittington 1354–1423
Lord Mayor of London

Where's your optimism, Bill? I haven't heard any officer
categorically rule out the chance of some downtime

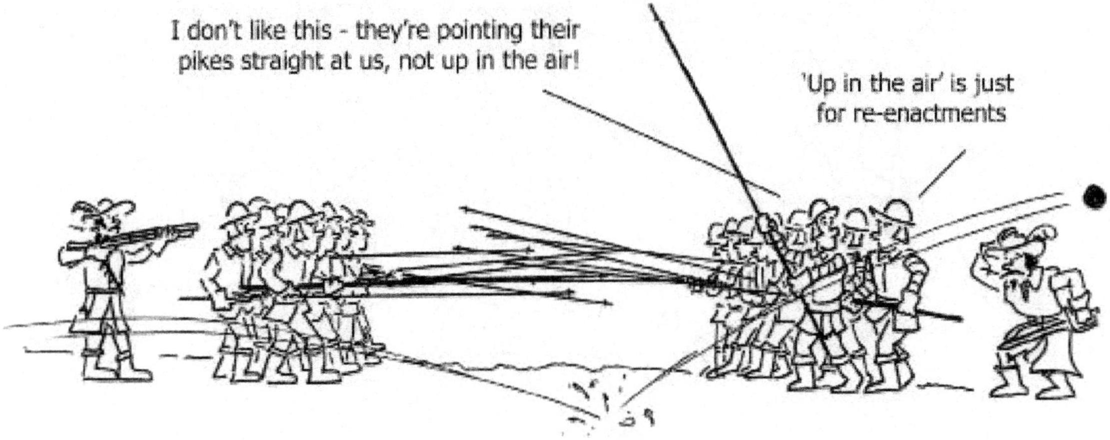
I don't like this - they're pointing their pikes straight at us, not up in the air!
'Up in the air' is just for re-enactments

Naseby

Chicken Chasseur

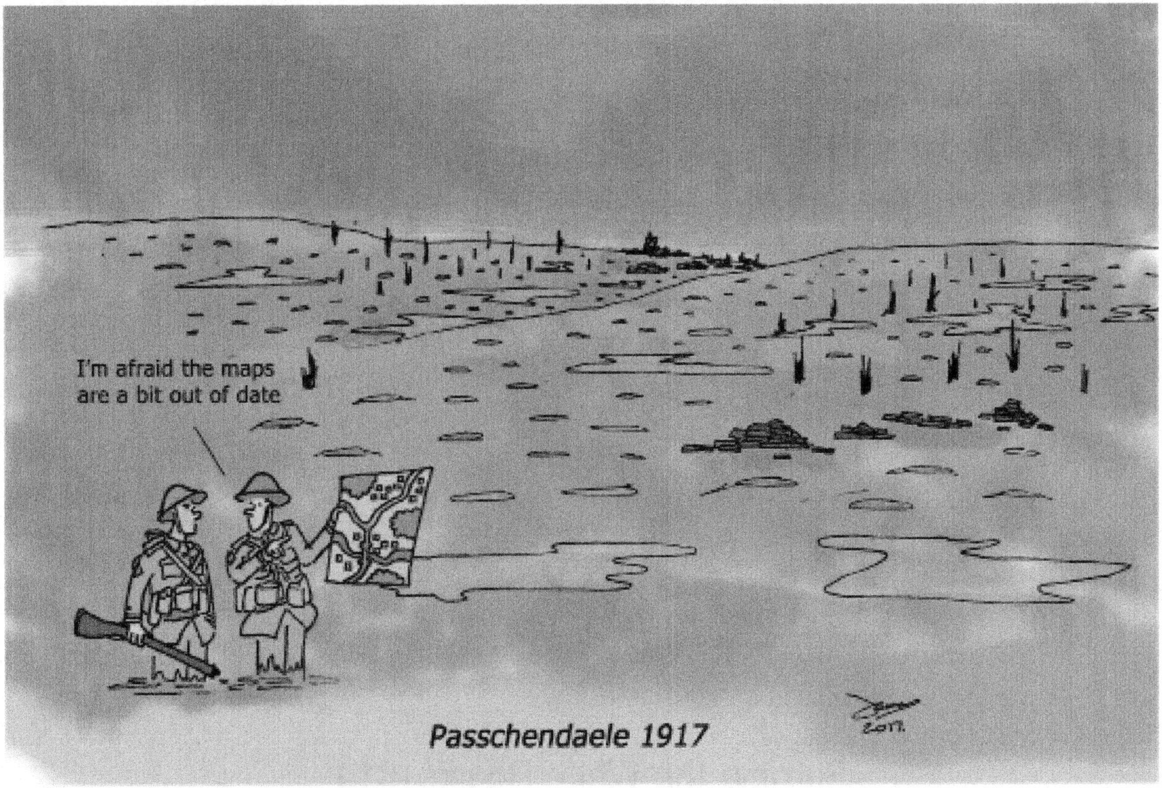
I'm afraid the maps are a bit out of date
2017.

Passchendaele 1917

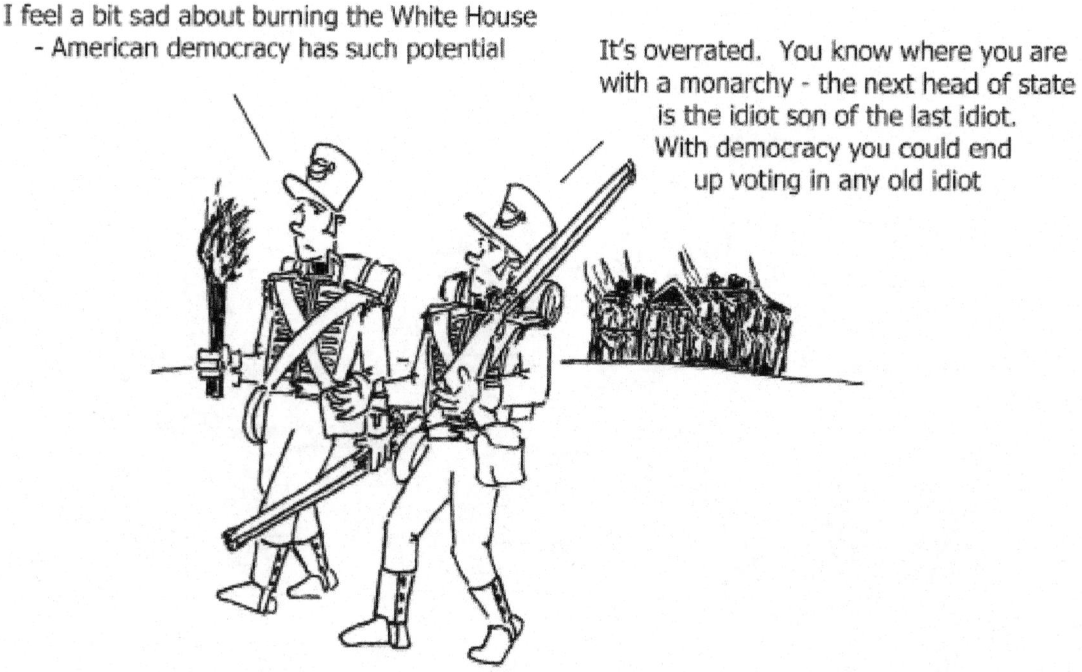
I feel a bit sad about burning the White House
- American democracy has such potential
It's overrated. You know where you are
with a monarchy - the next head of state
is the idiot son of the last idiot.
With democracy you could end
up voting in any old idiot

Burning the White House 1814

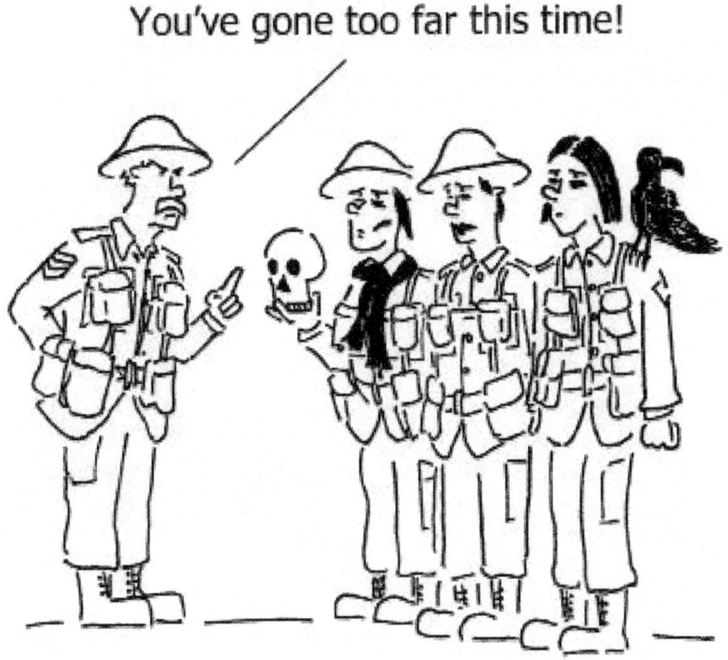
You've gone too far this time!

31st August 1944 - British 8th Army crosses the Gothic Line

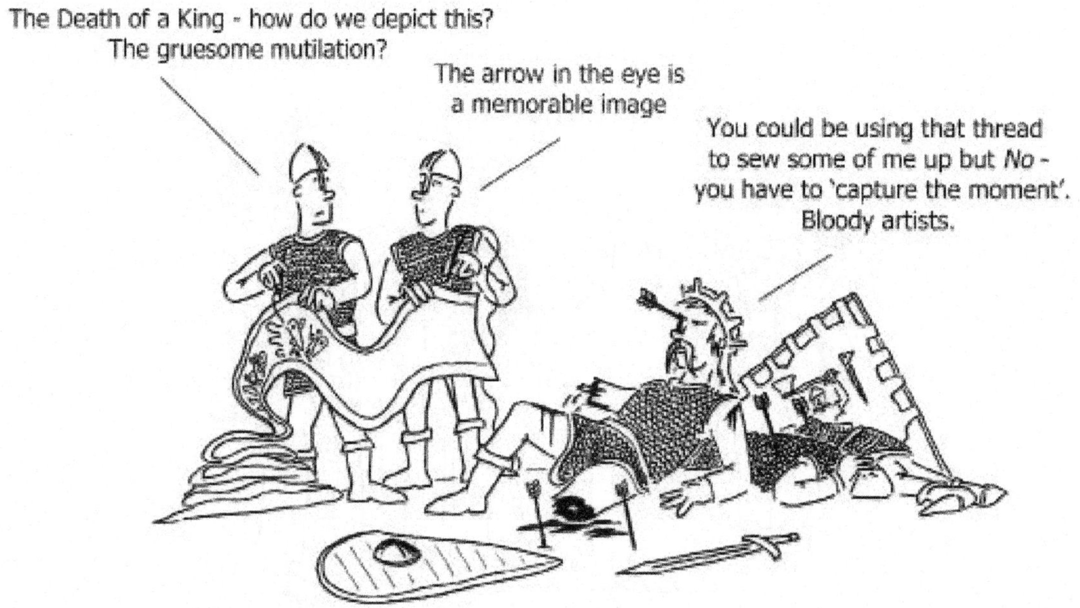
The Death of a King - how do we depict this? The gruesome mutilation?
The arrow in the eye is a memorable image
You could be using that thread to sew some of me up but *No* - you have to 'capture the moment'. Bloody artists.

Hastings 1066

Columbus Day

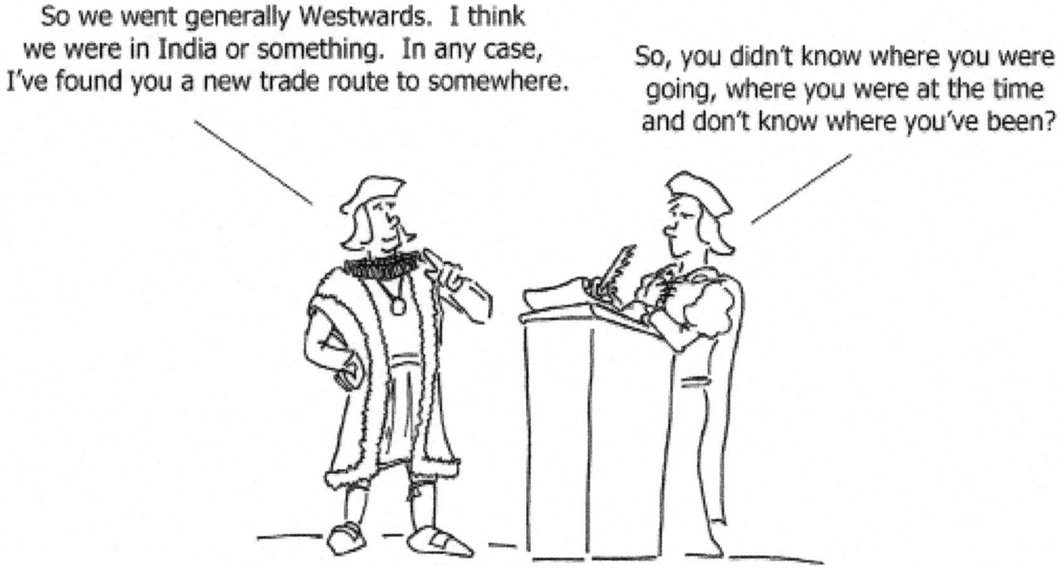
So we went generally Westwards. I think we were in India or something. In any case, I've found you a new trade route to somewhere.
So, you didn't know where you were going, where you were at the time and don't know where you've been?

And he did it all with someone else's money.

Odd sock drawer

Cartoons that don't have a home anywhere else

'Don't be scared if you don't fit in' sang The Raggy Dolls. These cartoons aren't so much in the reject bin as the unclassified pile. Some found homes, others remained unpublished (until now) but all are united by the fact that I enjoyed creating them and thought they belonged in this review.

They are certainly part of my 2017 and, as there isn't a recognised category for 'sheep, dogs, aliens, plumbers, zebras, babies, pirates, penguins and anthropomorphic sinks', this will be their new home.

Red sky at night
- Shepherd's delight

Red sky at morning
- Shepherd's warning

**Red sky at any time of day
& smell of burnt wool**
- Arsonist shepherd

Red dawn
- Communist incursion
- Your sheep will be confiscated and
distributed equally among the people

Red sky & red soil
- on Mars
- sheep asphyxiated

**Sky normal colour but filled with
unusually high number of angels**
- seek stable
- speak to employer re: holiday pay

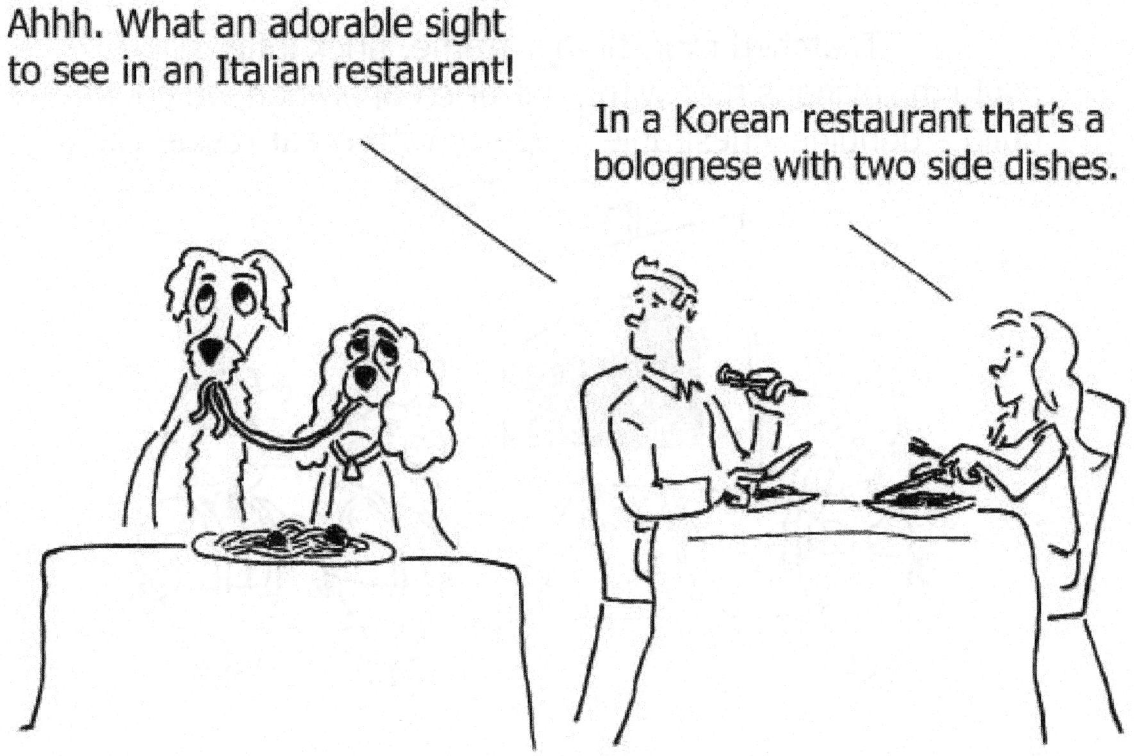
Ahhh. What an adorable sight to see in an Italian restaurant!
In a Korean restaurant that's a bolognese with two side dishes.

Thatched roof, timber frame, brick infill.
All I'm saying is that with a bit of co-operation we could
build a genuinely desirable property with great resale value

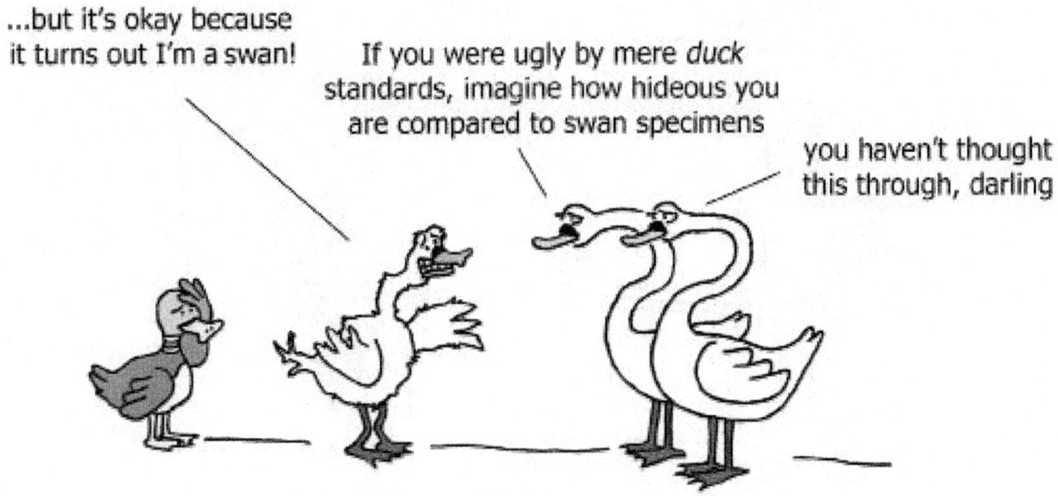
...but it's okay because
it turns out I'm a swan!
If you were ugly by mere *duck*
standards, imagine how hideous you
are compared to swan specimens
you haven't thought
this through, darling

The Ugly Duckling

No, he didn't fix the leak. This 'plumber' took drugs, punched some holes in the ceiling, stamped on my pet tortoise then ran off.

Ragnafragglerök

Whilst hugging, seeding and bursting forth from someone is one of
the most welcoming and loving gestures we can make in our society,
we have to be mindful of how this action is perceived by others

It's a cultural sensitivity thing

First Contact Committee

The dungarees were difficult.
They're a cape now.

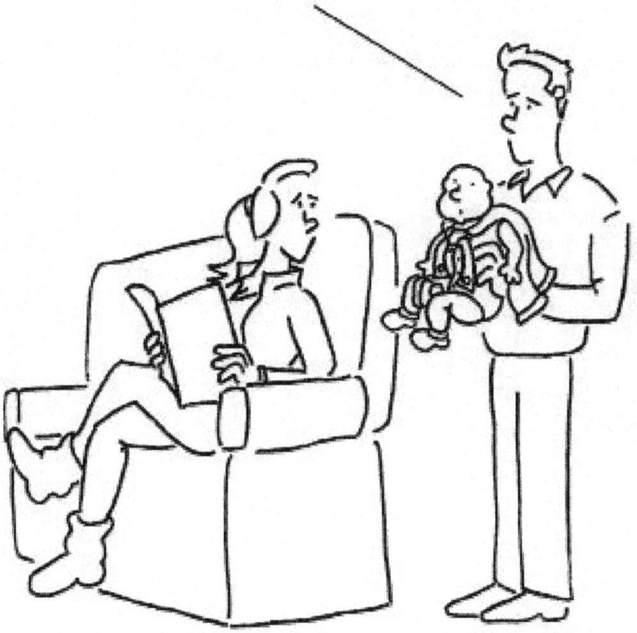

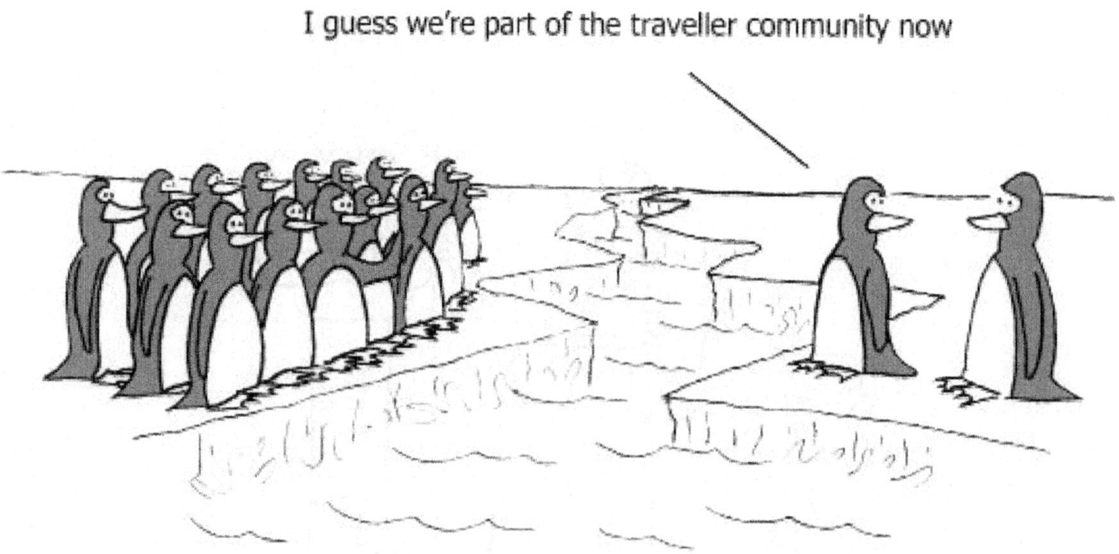
I guess we're part of the traveller community now

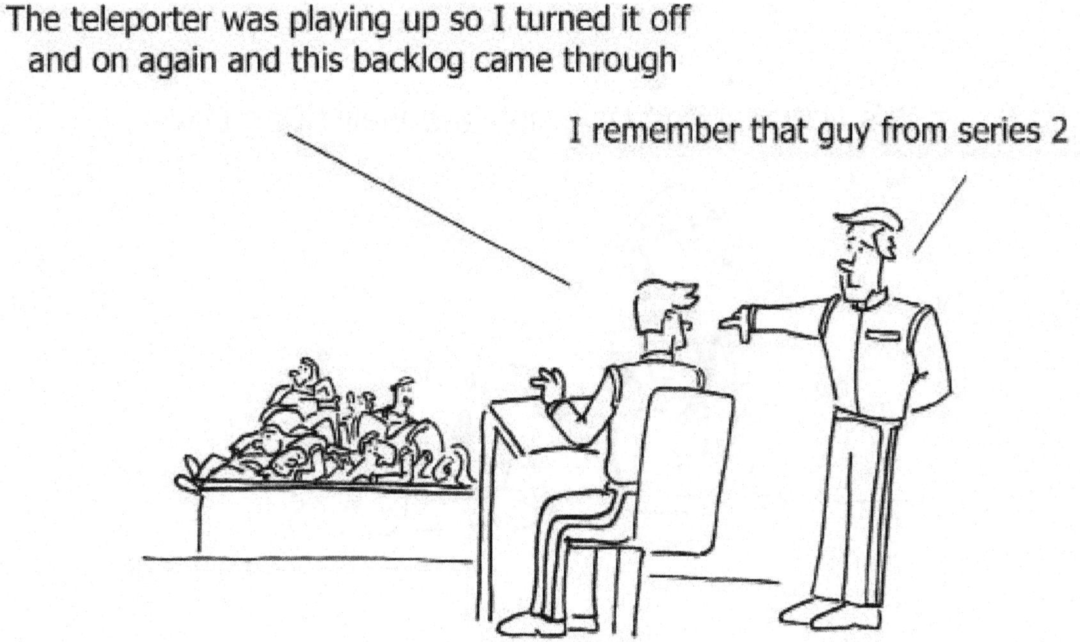
The teleporter was playing up so I turned it off and on again and this backlog came through
I remember that guy from series 2

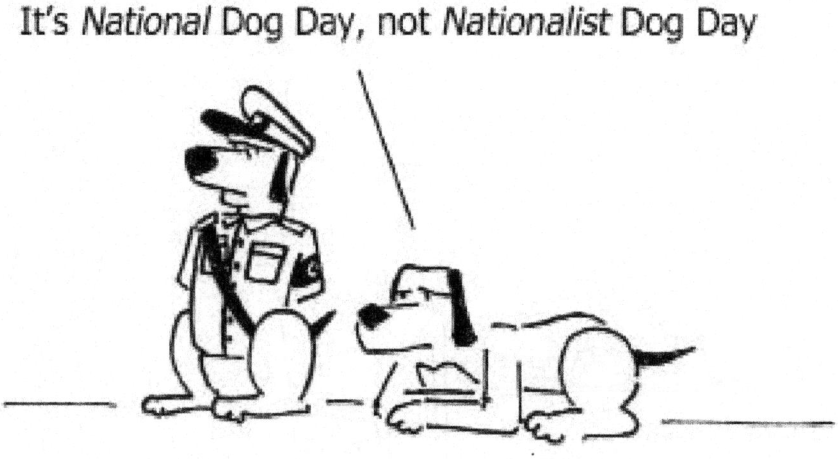
It's *National* Dog Day, not *Nationalist* Dog Day

So many toys... There must be *something* else we
could play all day that wouldn't ruin my back

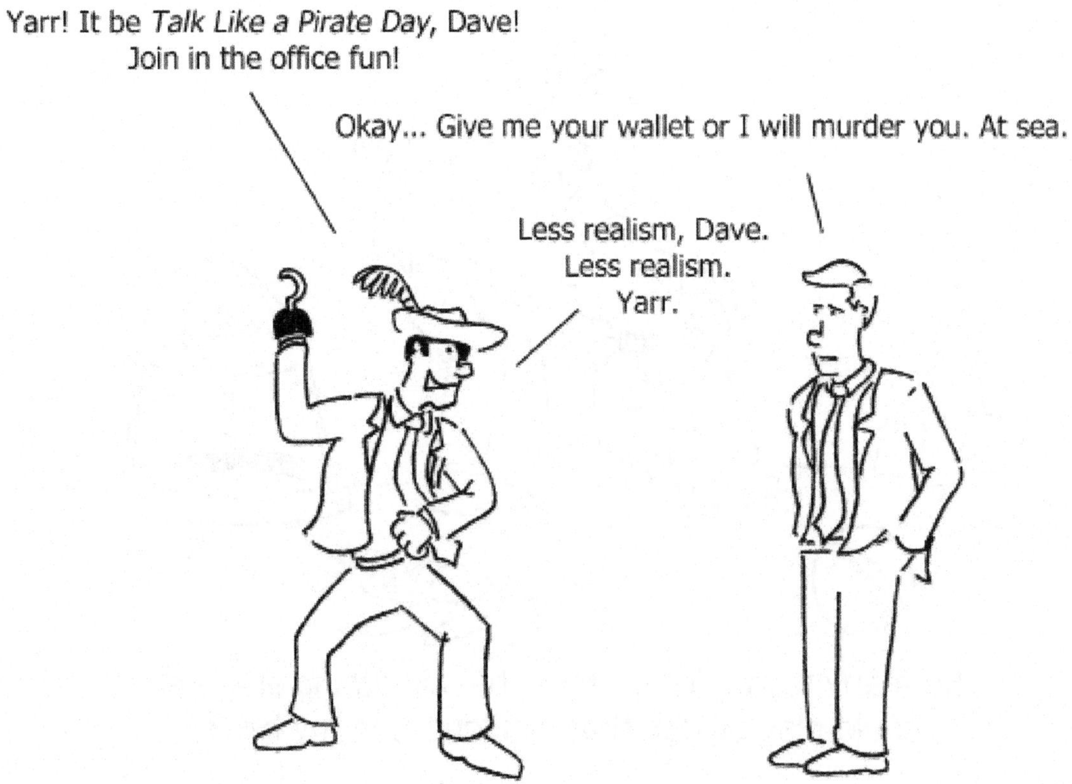
Yarr! It be *Talk Like a Pirate Day*, Dave!
Join in the office fun!
Okay... Give me your wallet or I will murder you. At sea.
Less realism, Dave.
Less realism.
Yarr.

It won't catch on you know

It didn't.

Let that sink in...

Find out more about books and services on
www.jamesmellorcreative.com
witter: @jamesdfmellor
Facebook: www.facebook.com/jamesmellorcreative

Thank you!

Lightning Source UK Ltd.
Milton Keynes UK
UKOW07f0938141117
312718UK00001B/1/P